Philosopher's Mental Models:
How to Think Like Lao Tzu, Descartes, Nietzsche, Kierkegaard, Plato, and More

By Peter Hollins,

Author and Researcher at petehollins.com

Table of Contents

CHAPTER 1: INTELLECTUAL DECISION-MAKING 7

USE THE POWER OF DOUBT	10
KEEP IT SIMPLE	22
LOOK FOR PATTERNS	33

CHAPTER 2: MORAL AND ETHICAL DECISION-MAKING 47

THE LAW OF KARMA	48
ACTING WITHOUT ACTING	59
CHESTERTON'S FENCE	70

CHAPTER 3: MEANING AND LONG-TERM DECISION-MAKING 85

NIETZSCHEAN ETERNAL RECURRENCE	86
PASCAL'S WAGER	95
ADOPTING A BEGINNER'S MIND	106

CHAPTER 4: PROBLEM-SOLVING IN DECISION-MAKING 119

VIA NEGATIVA—SUBTRACTION AS A PATH TO TRUTH	120
REMEMBER THAT THE MAP IS NOT THE TERRITORY	129
BURIDAN'S ASS	140

CHAPTER 5: EMBRACING THE UNKNOWN IN DECISION-MAKING — 153

TRANSFORMATIONAL CHANGE AND THE "VAMPIRE" ANALOGY — 154
TAKING THAT LEAP OF FAITH — 163
PLATO'S CAVE — 174

Chapter 1: Intellectual Decision-Making

"Choices are the hinges of destiny."

Edwin Markham

What makes a person's life a success?

Is it luck, genetics, upbringing, hard work, or temperament?

Some people seem to have been born with all the blessings and opportunities you could hope for, yet they don't succeed. Others seemingly start with nothing but reach unexpected levels of accomplishment. Why?

An often-overlooked life skill is decision-making and problem-solving. Every single one of us will face a life full of problems—big problems, trivial problems—but it's arguable that the presence and size of problems is less important than how we solve those problems.

In a way, we are all cursed with a staggering degree of freedom: At every moment there are countless paths ahead of us, each one branching off again to further decision points all throughout life. How are we to navigate our way through this maze?

We could focus on cultivating useful traits and characteristics (such as discipline or resilience) or tackle our limitations and bad habits on a psychological level (like low self-esteem or procrastination). These are all excellent things to focus on. In this book, however, we'll be exploring the skill of better decision-making itself, and how knowing how to choose wisely can greatly influence your success and well-being in life.

We'll do this by exploring a series of mental models that all have something to teach us about free will, choice, and knowledge. Which mental model is the best one? That's just it: *All* of them have (potential) value. By considering each mental model in turn, according to our purposes, we will be learning the meta-skill of using our own thinking modes as tools in a sophisticated toolkit.

Think of this book as a kind of theoretical microscope. Usually, microscopes have a revolving "objective lens" that you can turn so that you are peering at the same slide, but at different levels of magnification. This allows you to see the sample in very many different ways; what may be uninteresting and blurry under one lens may suddenly reveal itself to be fascinatingly clear using another.

As you read through each chapter, try to imagine that **each model is a lens through which to view your own problems, choices, and decision points in life, big and small**. Some of these lenses zoom right into the tiny details. Others zoom out and consider a broader, impressionistic view. Some explore the morality and wisdom of a decision. Others pull different things into focus: the utility, the logic, the practicality of a choice, and so on. Just like with a real microscope, switching through these different lenses may allow you to eventually find just the right one that brings everything into clear, brilliant focus.

As you read, bear in mind that not every mental model will be relevant or applicable. That said, with a little curiosity and open-mindedness, you may be surprised at just what you learn when you take a completely different perspective on the problem than you ordinarily would have!

Use the Power of Doubt

"Common sense is the best distributed commodity in the world, for every man is convinced that he is well supplied with it."

Renee Descartes

Today Descartes is considered one of, if not *the* most important, modern philosophers of all time, and his *cogito ergo sum* ("I think, therefore I am") rings a bell for most of us. Broadly, Descartes was ferociously concerned with what he could *know*—truly, once and for all, rationally. His branch of philosophy is called epistemology, which includes inquiries into the nature of knowledge itself.

- Where does knowledge come from?
- How can we say that we know things, and what does that really mean?
- If I perceive something as true, is that the same as it being true?
- What are beliefs? How are they different from knowledge, truth, habit, perception, or mere justification?
- If I wish to stay as closely aligned with what is objectively true as possible, what are the fundamental beliefs I can start with?

Descartes's thinking was heavily influenced by logic and mathematics, and his approach in the 1600s differed markedly from the European philosophers that came before him. **Descartes's work outlined a process for "thinking from scratch" and taking absolutely nothing for granted.** If we wished to think correctly and clearly, Descartes thought, we needed to seriously rid ourselves of all poor foundations (and everything built on those foundations) and start anew using only those propositions we had distilled for ourselves by pure reason. Descartes's work itself heralded a new attitude in philosophy in general, and a new commitment to take nothing for granted.

Descartes's primary tool? Doubt. Not emotional or psychological doubt, but philosophical and epistemological doubt—the willingness to question everything. The reward for such clear thinking, Descartes believed, was to arrive at something one could genuinely trust.

Descartes's "method of doubt" essentially consisted of throwing out anything he couldn't hold on to with 100 percent certainty. His famous *cogito ergo sum* was what he himself arrived at after much deliberation. If there was the phenomenon of someone thinking (or having experiences, asking questions, or experiencing doubts), he reasoned, then there must be *someone* to be having those doubts in the first place.

This mode of radical doubt tells us that the things we perceive, think, and believe are not automatically true. All this perceiving, thinking, and believing, however, is nevertheless taking place, and so there must at minimum be a consciousness doing it all. Thus, Descartes could conclude that he did, in fact, exist.

For most of us, Descartes's work may not seem especially innovative or groundbreaking, probably because we live a few hundred years into the era wholly characterized by the way of thinking he popularized. Many today believe that Descartes's conclusions were logically faulty and, furthermore, that his contribution to the Western canon has had many unfortunate ramifications, mainly Cartesian mind-body duality.

But even though he wrote hundreds of years ago, Descartes does have something to teach us moderns about making better quality decisions—indeed disciplining ourselves to have better quality thought processes in general. Without needing to reinvent the epistemological wheel like Descartes did, so to speak, **we can apply a little of his spirit of**

doubt as a counterbalance to our own biases, blind spots, and assumptions of "common sense."

Descartes outlines three "meditations," or thought experiments/arguments, that we can rework for our own ends. Descartes adopted a position of deliberate skepticism to navigate through each.

Retreat from the Senses

Can we trust the data we bring in from our senses? Is this information a reliable indication of reality? Here Descartes considers that the answer can sometimes be "no" ... and that this small amount of doubt means we can discount our senses as a solid method for acquiring knowledge. Why?

People are capable of "knowing" things incorrectly—for example, they can be fooled by optical illusions, they can be drunk and misperceiving, or they can be mad and hallucinating things that aren't there. Sensory perceptions, then, may *feel* like they're true, yet not be. This means that sensory perception in general is not trustworthy (at least, if our aim is to arrive at conclusive knowledge about the nature of reality).

Dreaming Hypothesis

But there's more. Descartes thought that the senses were unreliable, but so was our "sense" of understanding. You may say, for example, that you "know" that it is Tuesday today, and this is something you determine for yourself without recourse to your five senses. Consider, though, what happens when we dream. As we dream, our experience may have all the markers of genuine waking life without being so. We may have a dream in which we believe and think we know that it is Tuesday, when really, it's Wednesday. Dreams can feel so, so real, all while being 100 percent unreal. So, Descartes says, we can't rely on our own innate sense of "knowing," opinion, or belief either, since this could also lead us astray.

Imperfect Creator (or Evil Genius) Hypothesis

Descartes goes even further. What if there is an omnipotent being out there who is skillfully manipulating our entire sense of reality itself, even our sense of indubitable mathematical laws and principles? In Descartes's time, such a hypothesis ended up considering the nature and intentions of God, but more modern people may be prompted to consider hypotheticals of artificially created reality, simulacra of reality, or "brain in a vat" scenarios.

Our world today is more notably manipulated and controlled by vested interests than ever before, and people's perceptions of reality itself are interfered with at scale, whether that's by AI-generated images and video, fake news, and subtle or not-so-subtle fabrications ranging from photoshop to algorithms that funnel people into ideological bubbles that alter their entire worldview.

The point is, however, that we may be deceived on an even grander scale than we can by our own misperceptions and misapprehensions. If the things we "know" can be so successfully manipulated by external forces, then this, too, becomes an unreliable method for uncovering the truth of the objective world.

Where does all this leave us?

Descartes was interested in pure, 100 percent reliable knowledge, and he was a philosopher. You and me, on the other hand, may have many less-lofty goals: i.e., to be a little more rational, intellectually honest, and as objective as possible, given the very many caveats Descartes points out.

Consider Andrew, who is trying to make a decision almost as important as figuring out the nature of reality itself: He's trying to decide where to live. There are seemingly thousands of factors to consider, and Andrew feels overwhelmed. He's unable to make a decision, and he finds himself in a position not dissimilar from Descartes's—namely, the burning question "what do I *really know* here?"

Well, Descartes has helpfully already done the philosophical heavy lifting and convinced us all that we exist. But even with that fantastic foundation in place, the rest is still down to Andrew:

- He has always told himself that he wanted to live in a house with a big garden, having always lived in apartments, but how can he really **know** that he'll genuinely like having a garden?
- He is considering the mortgage options for various houses in different areas and is making plans according to what he believes he can afford ... but does he really **know** that he can afford it? How secure is his job, really?
- He has told himself time and time again that he doesn't want to live in neighborhood X because he's heard the crime is bad there, but when he thinks about it, why does he think this? Does he really **know** this is the case, or has he just guessed and made an assumption?
- Andrew **knows** that he should find a suitable place before winter because it will be hard to move when the weather is bad.

But does he have any evidence for thinking that?
- There are plenty of other beliefs and assumptions about what it means to buy a house, and who should do it, and why. Everyone **knows** that it's better to buy than rent, that it's fine to rent when you're younger, but if you're older, it's better to have your "own place," and that people who live in their "dream homes" are generally more successful in life than those who don't. In Andrew's social circle, for example, everyone knows that you can't live in a house that only has one bathroom. But is that actually true?

Now, the point of this kind of layperson's "method of doubt" is not to make you a neurotic ruminator and get stuck in overthinking. Rather, it's to gently **remind yourself that all the things you might currently be assuming are true . . . simply may not be**. Of course, they could be. But then again, they could not. The only way of discerning between the two is to actually stop and **ask yourself the question, "Do I have evidence that this is the case? Why do I think this?"**

Sometimes, we make poor decisions in life not because we are unintelligent but because we have failed to clearly distinguish between fact, opinion, perception, assumption, interpretation, and so on. Descartes tells us that any system of knowledge that we build on poor foundations will necessarily be poor also. To be better decision-makers, then, is not about building a better house, but making sure that you're not taking certain faulty foundations/assumptions as true when they aren't.

When Andrew sits down carefully and applies the clarifying solvent of doubt to every one of his thoughts and beliefs, he discovers with some relief that much of what he is taking as true is at best conjecture.

Furthermore, he realizes that a lot of his stress and overwhelm comes from buying into these assumptions and beliefs, and not from the process of choosing a house itself. This principle comes to us from cognitive behavioral therapy, or CBT, which tells us that we seldom react to reality itself, but rather our thoughts, reactions, interpretations, and conclusions *about* reality. Some problems can be solved within our frame of meaning, whereas others have to be solved by considering the frame of meaning itself and verifying for ourselves whether it is really accurate or helpful in any way.

Here are a few questions and prompts that can help you identify your own faulty assumptions and gaps in your own thinking. Descartes wanted to do this in order to arrive at a truly defensible model of reality, but we can follow a similar process in order to arrive at a worldview that is rational, healthy, adaptive, and genuinely useful for us. If you're feeling stuck and having a hard time making a decision, ask yourself:

What assumptions am I making here?

Take a closer look and don't take anything for granted. If you are telling yourself a "fact," then demand that you produce evidence for it. What support do you have for believing X, Y, and Z?

Often, we fail to realize that we have made assumptions in the first place—and these assumptions are the most dangerous, being the most stubborn and the most invisible. One major assumption for Andrew, for example, is that he should move somewhere at all. By focusing on the question "Where should I move?" he has jumped to a foregone conclusion that he should move at all.

Is what I'm thinking actually true?

All of us have a major cognitive blind spot: When we talk to ourselves, we simply take it for granted that what we are saying is in some sense how things really are. We lose sight of the filter we've laid onto reality and mistakenly think we are looking at reality itself. But often, what we are dealing with is not really reality, but rather a complex web of our own opinions, preferences, desires, fears, interpretations, etc.

Andrew realizes that his own reluctance to look for properties in neighborhood X has basically nothing to do with objective crime in that area, but rather with his own associations and opinions about the place. Sure, he still may choose not to live there, but by thinking through his beliefs carefully, he can correctly identify this impulse as a preference alone . . . and not a fact.

Am I deceiving myself?

Descartes was a mathematician (can you tell?) and found comfort and clarity in cold, hard logic. He was keenly aware of the fact that human beings are masters at lying to themselves. Their minds could create all manner of justifications, defenses, and reasons for ideas that could be just plain wrong. Physicist Richard Feynman once said, "The first principle is that you must not fool yourself, and you are the easiest person to fool."

In Andrew's case, a little honest self-reflection may reveal that his claim "I want to move to a nicer house" is not exactly accurate, since his deeper motivation is more like "I want others to see that I've bought a nice house, so they'll respect me and think I'm successful." Once he can honestly acknowledge that impulse for what it is, his decision-making process rapidly becomes simpler—the question of a garden or the number of bathrooms, for example, falls away completely.

Often, when we're making big life decisions, we barge ahead and look at the problem without ever stepping outside of our own small box of assumptions and limited understandings. But if we wish to be truly effective decision-makers, we need to take a page out of Descartes's book and get comfortable with throwing everything out—including all our beliefs about how best to solve problems—and starting afresh. That's because if we embark on a decision-making process but we use only a handful of unfounded assumptions and faulty beliefs, *all* of our decisions from that point, no matter how "good" they seem at the time, will be tainted.

Keep It Simple

"It is so vain to do more what can be done with less."

William of Ockham

In a way, Descartes's model allows us to "cut away" at everything in our thinking that is not strictly true or knowable. By doing so, we may (hopefully) be left with something that we have zero doubt about. In this chapter, we'll look at another kind of "mental razor" that helps us cut away at something else: unnecessary complexity.

Occam's razor, or the Law of Parsimony, is often given as "the simplest answer is usually the correct one," but this is actually not an accurate depiction of the principle. Rather, William of Ockham (the fourteenth-century philosopher who the principle is said to be named after) advises us to **adopt an explanation that depends on the smallest number of assumptions**. If you have two competing theories, for example, and both of them "explain" a phenomenon at hand, then the one that is less convoluted and which asks you to take fewer premises as given is likely to be the better theory.

Occam's razor is not a law written in stone, but a heuristic, i.e., a rule of thumb that points to a certain quality of reality—namely that it is parsimonious. "Simplicity" here is not a moral or aesthetic sense of things being lean or straightforward, but rather a theoretical simplicity. Consider the example of the Robert J. Hanlan quote that says, "Never attribute to malice what can be adequately explained by stupidity."

In fact, the above quote underlies what is often called "Hanlan's razor" since it so neatly captures a way to think about overly complex conspiracy theories—and how they may be more directly explained by human incompetence. For example, a famous celebrity makes the "devil horns" sign with both hands during an interview, and a flurry of online conjecture blooms around the question of whether this celebrity is actually a member of the illuminati or under the literal influence of Satan.

While this theory *could* be true, the fact is it depends on a huge number of assumptions—in fact, an entire web of preexisting conditions, many of which themselves are heavily contested as it is. An alternative theory is that the celebrity is just, well, stupid: the "devil horns" symbol is something they've seen people do, and so they've done it too, without giving a second thought to what they're doing. This theory requires far, far fewer assumptions. In fact, it's probably quite easy to imagine that a celebrity is especially prone to mimicking meaningless trends without understanding or caring what they mean!

For William of Ockham, if you introduced a theory to explain a phenomenon, but that theory itself contained its own unexplained phenomenon, then you haven't really gained any ground. In fact you may have invited additional complexity and room for error into your thinking.

In our example, many conspiracy theorists adopt overly complex explanations for phenomenon, and then in turn get sucked into the complexities of the explanation itself. So, in order for the theory "reptilian aliens are in control of the world" to be true, many other things need to be true.

It needs to be true that these aliens are all around us, but somehow hidden. If *that's* true, then this implies even more conspiracy and deception, and high intelligence and sophistication on the part of the lizard people. It implies that people know the secret but have been silenced (can they erase memories?) and that the truth is out there but deliberately being kept from us.

For the explanation to hold, we need a theory encompassing otherworldly shapeshifting and brainwashing technology, lizard people in the upper echelons of society, and a vast network of coordinated governmental efforts to keep all these machinations secret from the public, and so on and so on. We now have dozens of unexplained phenomena, rather than just one.

It's easy enough to mock conspiracy theorists, but **many of us think in precisely the same way when we get trapped in overly complex "explanations" for things that only require smaller, more provisional descriptions**. For a host of reasons, we may jump to very exotic explanations for fairly mundane problems, or seek solutions that are really too big for the problems they are attempting to solve. The more emotional we feel about a problem, and the less information we have about it, the more likely we are to jump to conclusions. Take a look at a few examples.

- Your printer won't work. Before angrily concluding, "It's a piece of junk. I probably have to throw the whole thing away!" first consider whether it simply isn't plugged in or connected. Then move on to more damning diagnoses!
- If a doctor encounters a patient with a stomachache, he is likely to first consider overeating, a simple allergy, or heartburn before he considers a rare pancreatic cancer or an intestinal parasite you can

only acquire in the jungles of Papua New Guinea.
- You're out walking one day in the street, and from afar you spot a colleague from work. They turn around and walk the other way. You could conclude that they secretly hate you along with everyone else in the office . . . or you could start with an explanation that requires fewer assumptions: They probably didn't see you.

The simplest solution isn't always the best one, but it often has a higher chance of being so, if for no other reason that simple solutions are easier to actually implement. Sometimes anxiety can cause us to overthink and look at a potential problem so that we see something that is far scarier and complex than it really is. A problem always contains the element of the unknown. If we're not careful, we can end up projecting all sorts of assumptions into that void of the unknown. In other words, a rustle in the bushes can be created by anything our imaginations can conjure up!

Using Occam's razor is a clever way to make sure that this kind of fear and assumption is not driving your decision-making. People who cling to wild conspiracy theories do so not because they're unintelligent or lacking information, but rather because they are engaging in a very emotional way with the data they do have. They are experiencing extreme suspicion, fear, doubt, and anger, but are unable to see how this emotional response is influencing their ability to think rationally. In the same way, anger and frustration may make you want to solve your printer problem by throwing it out the window, when the more rational response is to calmly troubleshoot one step at a time.

How can we apply this principle/approach in our own decision-making?

Step 1: Clarify the problem you're trying to solve.

Step 2: Identify all the possible explanations for the problem that you can think of.

Step 3: Consider each alternative's assumptions and its overall simplicity, and then rank the possible explanations.

Step 4: Start with the simplest explanation or the one that requires fewest assumptions.

Step 5: If that isn't helping, then move on to the next, and so on.

Realistically, few of us are going to be sitting down with a pen and paper and identifying all the different possible explanations for a problem we're facing—life is often far too complicated for that! More commonly,

Occam's razor is a principle we can incorporate into our overall decision-making process. After all, the way we make decisions and the way we solve problems overlap considerably and are influenced in turn by how we think about the situation, what we know and don't know, and our own goals and intentions.

You can blend this process, for example, with the method of doubt introduced in the previous section. As you ask, "What do I know for certain here?" you are also shining a light on various assumptions—these assumptions are pointing to explanations or ways of understanding that could possibly be simpler and more direct.

Sometimes an option seems obvious to us, but when we look more closely, we realize that we've actually skipped ahead mentally and attached ourselves to a solution that is far more complicated than it needs to be. The reasons we do this are, as we've seen, more about emotion and habit than they are about objective, rational fact.

Maybe you're doing some DIY on your house and fixing some wiring or plumbing. But when you switch on the light or turn on the faucet, it doesn't work. Why? **Rather than invent new reasons and explanations, consider instead**

that some of your existing assumptions are in fact the problem. In other words, the situation is showing you that your current way of thinking of the problem is not correct or adequate. Take a look at every one of your assumptions and double check them in turn.

In "electrical troubleshooting," you observe only the smaller circuit you are working on before concluding that the problem is bigger and system-wide. You first look for visible signs of trouble before functional ones (Is the cable damaged? Plugged in? Is it on fire?). You start to think of causes, and set up some conditional if/then statements—"If I plug X and Y in, then Z happens, but if I plug X alone in, then Z doesn't happen." You consider each premise, assumption, and belief in turn before considering them in combination, and so on.

Life is usually more complex than an electrical problem, but the principles are the same. Let's imagine the situation of Ava, who has a problem with her boyfriend, and apply the process step by step.

Step 1: Clarify the problem you're trying to solve.

Not as easy as it first seems! Ava is upset and uneasy, but it takes some clear thinking to identify exactly why. After mulling over it calmly and clearly, and writing out some notes in a journal, she concludes that the problem is that her boyfriend seems distant and uncommunicative with her after a weekend they spent camping with another couple they're friends with.

Step 2: Identify all the possible explanations for the problem that you can think of.

This step is easier for Ava, and she already has several explanations (conspiracy theories?) about why this problem is happening, what it means, and therefore what the solution is. Here are a few she writes in her journal:

- Her boyfriend is angry with her for drinking too much on the camping trip, but he doesn't want to say anything because he doesn't want to appear controlling, because Ava has already expressed to her boyfriend many times that she broke up with her last boyfriend because she felt he was controlling.
- Her boyfriend is gradually losing interest in her and is simply drifting away; on the camping trip he saw the other happy couple and got to thinking how he didn't share that with Ava.
- Her boyfriend is acting just the same as he always does, but Ava herself no longer feels that his communication style is working for

her, and might want to chat with him about it, or possibly break up.

Step 3: Consider the assumptions inherent in each alternative explanation, and its overall simplicity, and then rank the possible explanations.

Ava looks through each alternative explanation and realizes that *every single one of them* rests on a long string of assumptions, guesses, and conjectures. This is a realization in itself: Things may feel very real and serious yet may be completely unsubstantiated. This means she can actually skip the step where she is weighing up all the alternatives, and understand that none of her ways of thinking about the problem are really supported by much evidence.

What kind of explanation might be the simplest? What would it look like to have zero assumptions about this situation? After thinking about it for a while, Ava realizes that the simplest, most straightforward way of thinking about this "problem" is to acknowledge, "I don't actually know what my boyfriend is thinking."

From here, she could do a few things. She could decide to forget about the whole incident. She could simply talk to him and see what he says. But one thing she knows she really *shouldn't* do is stew over what her boyfriend might be thinking, what that means, and what that in turn could imply, and so on and so on. For Ava, Occam's razor is not just an intellectual weapon—it's something that helps her cut away unnecessary drama and self-induced distress.

Of course, life as a rule is *not* simple, and Occam's razor teaches us that even the assumption "fewer assumptions are always better" is sometimes not true! There are occasions where the best way to think about something is more complex than you'd expect. Another limitation should be clear from Ava's example: We can only ever work with the information we have. If we don't have much information, then all our theories and ideas are likely to be as weak as each other.

The strength of pulling out Occam's razor, however, is that it reminds us that so **much of the complexity we see before us may not actually be in the problem itself, but in our way of thinking about it.** A few great questions to ask:

- Does the level of complexity of my thinking about this problem match the complexity of the problem itself?
- Am I answering a question or solving a problem in a way that actually just

introduces further problems and questions?
- Am I mind reading and making assumptions about other people's intentions, goals, perceptions, and interpretations?
- Have I confused a personal need, desire, expectation, or fear with an explanation of the problem?

Look for Patterns

"Finding patterns is the essence of wisdom."

Dennis Prager

If we take Descartes's approach, we will ensure that we are trimming away all but the things we know for certain are true. If we apply Occam's razor, we will also be able to cut out unfounded assumptions and complexities that at best don't help and at worst actually hinder our thinking process.

In this chapter, we'll consider things from a slightly different perspective. Sometimes the situations we're trying to digest, the problems we're trying to solve, and the decisions we're trying to weigh up are not linear. It's not a question of simply asking if something is true or not, but rather a question of relationships—i.e., how different factors and variables interact with one another.

This is especially the case for problems, decisions, and situations that are large and rather shapeless, as well as those that don't have an objective basis. "Is there a monster under my bed?" is a problem that can be swiftly dealt with using the scientific method and a little bravery. But **the question "What should I do with my life?" requires a different tack entirely. There is no true or false.**

Here's where Venn diagrams can help. Most of us know what Venn diagrams are, but few of us appreciate how powerful they can really be. By representing certain ideas, facts, considerations, factors, etc. visually like this, we can see at a glance certain relationships that may otherwise not be apparent to us. It may seem like overstating the case, but Venn diagrams are a good example of how *the way we process information heavily influences what* we can process, and what we "see" when considering the data in front of us.

Very simply, Venn diagrams are graphic representations of the relationship between two factors—almost always their overlap or commonality. Without having to express it verbally, a Venn diagram can show the relationship between, for example, the skills required for two different jobs. Job A requires a set of skills represented by a circle encompassing these competencies, Job B requires a set of its own skills, contained within its own circle, and where the two circles overlap, we can see the handful of skills that both Job A and Job B share. At a glance we can see everything that the two jobs have in common, as well as those things that are exclusive to each job alone.

This simple concept can be made more interesting and more complex by adding more circles. Check out this funny one from Matt Shirley:

In just one image, we can see *dozens* of clever relationships between the different factors. Though the diagram above is obviously a joke, it is also a sound example of the principle. A

Venn diagram shows its true value when it quickly conveys certain relationships and areas of overlap that would otherwise require lots of explanation, graphs, or tables, or illuminates points of similarity where you didn't think there were any.

John Venn was a philosopher and logician who gave his name to this kind of diagram in the late 1800s, even though he was not technically the first to experiment with this kind of graphical representation. He used such diagrams to capture and easily explain basic set theory, principles of probability, and other ideas in math, statistics, and computer science.

But Venn diagrams are also amazing decision-making tools to have in your inventory for all those questions and concerns that are so vast and multifaceted that you feel as though you're completely lacking direction. Taking the time to pause and construct a Venn diagram from scratch can be surprisingly illuminating.

So, what kinds of problems can a Venn diagram help with?

Situations in life can often seem complicated and muddled but can be clarified if all your ideas can be categorized so that some of that detail can be boiled down and simplified. If you're trying to make a decision that requires a careful weighing up of two options or possible paths, a Venn diagram can help, as it can if you're needing to capture many separate dimensions in an easy-to-understand way. Let's take a look at a simple example:

You're choosing between one university program and another. You use a Venn diagram to help you see which features each option exclusively possesses, as well as which features belong to both. By identifying what is common to both options, you can effectively remove these factors from your decision-making process, since both choices amount to the same outcome as far as these variables are concerned.

You could even do a further Venn diagram where you map the features of each university against the features you are most seeking in your further education, then analyze the overlap. Again, you can discount all the features of each university if they don't actually appear in your own circle of "must haves."

After making this Venn diagram and perhaps a few other notes, you should be left with "data" that has been cut in interesting and illuminating ways: You may see only those features of each university that actually matter to you, as well as those that you will have access to regardless.

By going through this process, you streamline your thinking and prevent yourself from getting too caught up in details of the decision-making process that are actually not relevant or important. For example, University A boasts an impressive gym on campus and plenty of exciting sporting opportunities, but the truth is that the sporting aspect is just not that important for the goals you've set for yourself. What's more, University B has a gym and sports provision nearly as good! What this means is that the Venn diagram is helping you take what *feels* like a daunting situation with an overwhelming number of variables and trim things down to what really matters.

One excellent way to use Venn diagrams is to help you find direction and clarity in some of those bigger life decisions, such as:

What should your college major be?

What kind of job should you train or apply for?

What kind of lifestyle do you actually want for yourself?

What should you even be doing with your life?

Should you date or marry this person? (Or even break up or divorce?)

For these kinds of problems and decisions, you'll need to take the time to gather all the information you have and compare it closely with your own goals, limitations, personal strengths, dreams, fears, and so on. Very simply, all of life can be represented by a single Venn diagram: There is the circle of what you want, and the other circle of what is possible for you. The space between is the space where you should focus (and indeed it's the only place where you *can* meaningfully focus!).

Always remember: **If you can find a pattern, you can find insight**. If you can begin to see the connections and relationships between things, then you are closer to making a decision or finding a solution (which is really nothing more than a relationship or pattern that you simply haven't seen yet).

Take a look at the following diagram from a CNBC article by management author Suzy Welch. It includes three overlapping sets: skills, interests, and opportunities, and in between, the sweet spot that she calls the "area of destiny."

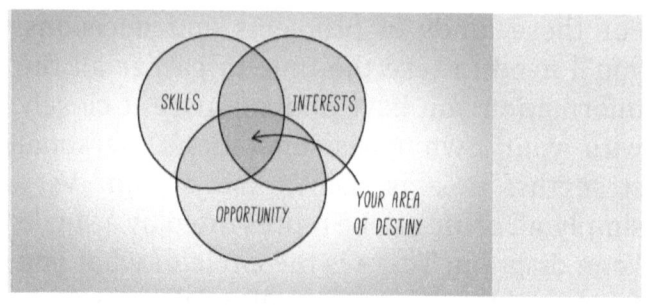

Step 1: Identify skills, abilities or characteristics

First begin by identifying your skills or valuable characteristics and traits (this will depend somewhat on what your overall decision or question is). Welch recommends being as specific as possible, and being as comprehensive as possible, too. Include everything you can think of (many people will underappreciate a certain skill they have precisely because it comes so naturally to them).

That said, if you are trying to figure out what course of study to embark on or what area of work to pursue, you want these skills to not be limited to any pre-existing path or role you have for yourself. So, you could list things like writing skills, negotiation, mediation, detail orientation, good listening, patience, quick to learn, able to speak Spanish, a comfortable team player, and so on.

Step 2: Identify your goals, values, and what you want

The next circle is for your interests and preferences—i.e., what you want. Again, how you complete this circle will depend on how you're framing your question/problem/decision. You may decide that it's more appropriate to list out the values and principles you most want to live by (or at least apply to this particular situation), or you may find yourself focusing on a short- or long-term goal with a defined outcome.

For many people, it can be pretty interesting to realize that this circle and the previous one do not overlap in quite the way they thought it might. It's not necessarily true that we will enjoy the things we're good at, or the corollary, we might not be any good at the things we most enjoy doing! People can sometimes find themselves making poor life decisions because of muddled thinking in this area. They believe that if they're good with figures and can work with money easily, for example, then that will somehow translate to enjoying being an accountant or actuary. But is that true? (Note how the Venn diagram, just like our other two mental models, also has its way of subtly challenging our inbuilt assumptions.)

On the other hand, some people have been led to believe that if only they have enough passion and interest for a particular route in life, then that will somehow translate into concrete aptitude for that thing. But is that true? If you've ever met an enthusiastic but nevertheless mediocre hobbyist, you'll already know that it isn't always as straightforward as that!

In our example, you might realize that although you're an expert at mediation and communicating your way out of conflict, you don't actually *enjoy* doing so. While you may enjoy being useful at work and having your skills appreciated, on reflection this is not something that inspires or interests you on a deeper level.

Step 3: Identify your opportunities

If you love speaking Spanish and are really good at teaching others to speak it, that's one thing. But if you happen to live in an area where everyone speaks Spanish already, there's probably not enough overlap between the three circles to genuinely consider "Spanish teacher" as a life path . . . unless you are willing to move, that is.

In this circle, you want to do a broad survey of the opportunities that are available in your environment. Again, sometimes just taking the time to list these down in black and white can open your eyes to aspects of a situation you hadn't considered before. Try to be specific, honest, and thorough—most of us have more resources at our disposal than we think.

Include in this circle any people who are able to help and mentor, any unmet needs in the market, any potential gaps you could fill or exploit, problems you could solve for others, gifts you could offer, solutions you could share, and so on. What is available to you, and what might be more available with just a little effort on your part? Here you are looking for the neatest, most obvious fit between who you are and the world you live in (or, for that matter, the world you want to live in).

This three-step approach may seem simple, but don't underestimate it; used properly, it can help you uncover new areas of possibility, not to mention help you let go of ideas and assumptions that are impractical or simply unfounded.

Often, big decisions come with common advice like "follow your dreams," which, on closer reflection, may not really lead you down the right path. We can imagine that finding the common space between "interests" and "abilities" is useful, but it will not quite be right unless there is a concrete way to connect that to the real-world environment you actually find yourself in.

The *ikigai* concept (Japanese for "reason for being") is an interesting expansion/variation on this theme. There are four aspects here, with the additional circle of "what the world needs." Some jobs may be virtuous and beneficial for mankind, but difficult or poorly paid. Others may be well paid but make no use of your natural talents and gifts. Below is the *ikigai* Venn diagram that summarizes the relationship between all these various aspects. You can use it to help you construct your "dream job" from scratch, or you can use it retrospectively, almost to diagnose areas of concern or potential improvement in the job you currently have. Either way, the power comes in looking for those previously unseen patterns.

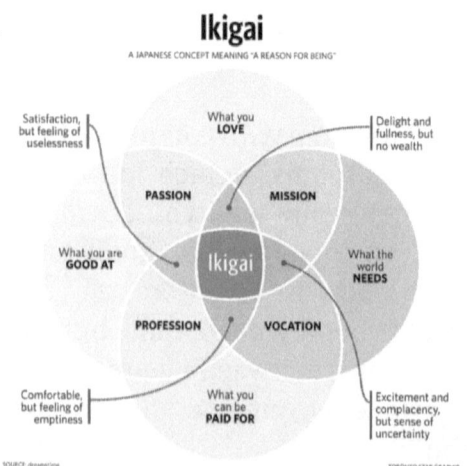

Summary

- Descartes was a philosopher concerned with knowledge and what could be known. He proposed "thinking from scratch" and taking absolutely nothing for granted. He suggested epistemological doubt and questioning everything. Healthy skepticism can counterbalance the biases, blind spots, and assumptions of unexamined "common sense."
- We cannot automatically trust our senses, feelings, opinions, perceptions, beliefs, or hopes. We also may be deceived by ourselves or others. All the things you might currently be assuming are true simply may not be.
- We seldom react to reality itself, but rather our thoughts, reactions, interpretations, and conclusions *about* reality. Ask what assumptions you're making, what evidence you really have, and whether you may be deceiving yourself.
- Occam's razor is a heuristic that advises us to adopt an explanation that depends on the smallest number of assumptions. Try not to let strong emotions distort your thinking and make things overly complicated.

- Rather than invent new reasons and explanations, consider instead that some of your existing assumptions are in fact the problem. In other words, the situation is showing you that your current way of thinking of the problem is not correct or adequate.
- *The way* we process information heavily influences *what* we can process. Venn diagrams can help us understand relationships between different variables and consider their overlap.
- If you can find a pattern, you can find insight. If you can begin to see the connections and relationships between things, then you are closer to making a decision or finding a solution.

Chapter 2: Moral and Ethical Decision-Making

Descartes was a mathematician, and Venn was a logician. William of Ockham was a theologian and Catholic apologist, but the principle for which he is best known is one that concerns his natural philosophy and logical arguments, not his faith. All of this is to say that when it comes to wanting to make decisions that feel logical, rational, and intellectually sound, it makes sense to turn to those theories and mental models that come to us from the world of philosophy and science.

However, doing the "right" thing is not always the "right" thing!

In this chapter, let's take a look at all of life's problems and big decisions using an entirely different set of lenses. We'll consider the

Buddhist law of karma and how it helps us understand the web of cause and effect that creates and sustains our life, and how to choose an action according to its consequence.

We will also explore the analogy called "Chesterton's fence," which can help us become more aware of all those consequences of our actions that may currently be invisible to us. Finally, we'll look at the ancient Chinese concept of *Wu Wei*, which considers the principle of action in its reverse—i.e., what we can do by choosing not to do anything at all. Let's dive in.

The Law of Karma

"Karma is the eternal assertion of human freedom . . . Our thoughts, our words, and deeds are the threads of the net which we throw around ourselves."

Swami Vivekananda

Karma may be one of the most widely known but also most widely misunderstood topics in Buddhism. It comes from the Sanskrit word for "action." **Karma is said to be a principle describing how actions naturally grow out of thoughts and feelings, and how those actions themselves then create our world through the power of cause and effect.** Over time our thoughts and feelings become actions, and when repeated often enough, those actions become habits, and a whole world of effects and results springs from that.

Moral philosophy and ethics take a completely different view on the big questions of our lives, and so offers a different approach to making decisions and solving problems. In the Western imagination, karma is sometimes simply associated with a basic idea of "justice," but the principle is far more complicated. For Buddhists, karma is the idea that **everything in this world that exists right now came into being because of a particular cause**. Some of those causes will be human behavior. In this model of the world, virtuous actions bring about happiness and harmony, and unvirtuous actions bring about suffering.

If you plant a seed in the ground, and all the conditions are just right, the seed will sprout and grow. In the same way, if you plant the "seed" of anger or desire or fear in yourself, and the conditions are just right, that seed will sprout and bring about real consequences in the world around you. If all the necessary conditions align without opposition, a particular effect is inevitable. Of course, humans have the freedom to resist certain actions, to cultivate others, and so on.

The seed has a natural inclination to grow. We as humans may also come into the world with natural inclinations—our karmic urge—to take this or that action. This urge is like momentum, like a habit that has been learned over time. It pushes us to behave in certain ways when we encounter certain conditions in our environment. For example, someone cuts us off in traffic and the urge to anger springs up in us. We can understand all our actions as resulting from the interaction between our karmic urge and the environmental conditions we face.

In one sense, the "law" of karma can sound very deterministic. But it's only when we understand all the influences on our behavior that we have a hope of mastering ourselves—or detaching from our habitual behaviors entirely. Understood this way, karma is the urge or compulsion to act in a particular way, and not the effect or consequence of that action. Our karmic urges can be physical and behavioral, but they can also be social, emotional, even mental, if we understand thoughts as a kind of "internal behavior"!

Karma, good or bad, is what keeps us chained to the cycle of samsara—the endless death and rebirth of life. Though a full discussion of karma is well beyond the scope of this book (it is, after all, not so much a mental model as an entire branch of philosophy), there are a few basic concepts we can use to improve our decision-making:

- Small actions can bring large results, and vice versa. But you always "reap what you sow." You cannot sow rice and expect to harvest barley.
- Karma is yours and yours alone—the cause for one action cannot transfer itself to an effect somewhere else, and a person who takes an action cannot have the results of that action taken from them.
- By the same token, karmic actions don't just go away by themselves. We must either face their results, take new and better actions, or find a way to rid ourselves of the "habit."
- We are beholden to the rules of cause and effect whether we are conscious of the actions we are taking or not.

In the West, **we might think of karma in cognitive behavioral terms: With enough conditioning and unconscious habit, we may fall into automatic behavior that shapes our world.** Our patterns of thinking, feeling, and behavior become an impetus all their own and continue to bring about certain results. Some of these results may be very far-reaching indeed, with some believing that karma can carry over even from previous lifetimes, and even that countries, nations, and civilizations can incur their own forms of generational karma that are very embedded and lasting indeed.

What does all of this have to teach us about making better decisions in our lives, here and now? From the karmic frame of reference, acting is not especially a moral choice—each of us is continually faced with an infinite number of choices, and the results are neither punishment nor reward—they merely follow as a natural and predictable consequence.

Nevertheless, blessed with reason and consciousness, human beings can step back and take a more considered look at their choices, not just those that impact them in the immediate moment, but those with broader consequences. Before you act, you can ask yourself:

What are the natural consequences of this action? Not just immediately or tomorrow or in a week, but many months and years and even decades from now. If a decision is big enough, consider how it impacts people even after you yourself have passed away.

Will this choice bring you closer to your goals or further away? Will this choice create more harmony, health, and prosperity for you, or will it undermine all those things and bring unhappiness? Again, consider not only how it impacts you but others around you.

Will this choice reinforce your identity as the sort of person you actually want to be? In other words, is it the kind of decision that the person you want to be would make?

How does this decision feel in your body? Does the thought of a particular action bring tension, fear, uneasiness, rage, and so on? Or does it create a feeling of well-being, balance, calm, and safety?

If you are faced with two or more decisions, paths, options, or attitudes, ask yourself which one you want to feed and grow with your attention and your choices. You may only see adversity and discomfort as potential choices. But could you choose to deliberately find the blessing in those limited options anyway, and choose to water the "seed" of resilience and patience?

Remember always that when you choose an action, you are also choosing its consequences. Then, ask yourself: Do you *want* to choose those consequences? Sometimes we act out of wanting to avoid or escape something without too much thought of what lies in the future because of that choice. In the Buddhist understanding, such action is likely to incur negative karma.

In life, all action carries consequences, including choosing not to act. This is not a cause for anxiety or worry, however. Rather, as the quote at the opening of this section explains, karma is "the eternal assertion of human freedom." At every moment, we are creating the world around us through a complex net of cause and effect. Every choice we make opens us up to a different set of possibilities. Our freedom, then, can be a terrifying freedom!

For the Buddhists, samsara is the eternal round of cause and effect, of death and rebirth, and of attachment and suffering. One way to remove yourself from samsara and your karmic impetus is to attain enlightenment, detach, and transcend. On a more mundane level, however, **we can achieve a lot simply by becoming more aware of the greater karmic and moral implications of everything we do, think, and say.**

Applying Cause-and-Effect Thinking to Problem-Solving

The law of karma can help us take a different view on our actions (and yes, thoughts, feelings, and perceptions are a kind of *internal* action), but we can also use the cause-and-effect mental model to help us better understand things from the other direction—i.e., to help us identify the root causes of the problems around us.

According to this model, every effect we see in the world once had a cause—or many causes. By understanding the factors that go into bringing a situation about, we deepen our comprehension of our life situations and expand our consciousness and sense of control.

We no longer merely react to problems as they spring up, but become empowered to engage with them in a deeper way. When we think of "morality," it's easy to imagine that things are either a good idea or a bad idea, right or wrong. In truth, everything around us evolves as a **process**. Knowing how the process unfolds helps us make better decisions and intervene when not-so-good decisions have already occurred and crystallized themselves as apparent problems.

The irony is that this kind of "moral" decision-making and problem-solving can help us take strong emotion out of the equation—we need not get upset, avoid, escape, lay blame, or feel shame or anger at ourselves. We simply take a step back and become curious about how and why things have developed as they have.

Here's a step-by-step problem to illustrate how simple the cause-and-effect way of thinking can be.

Step 1: Identify the problem

Look around you and try to be clear about exactly what is not quite right at the moment. Be precise and put proper labels on things.

For example, you notice it's 11 a.m. and you're at work with an awful headache. You're in a foul mood and you want to kill your colleague working at the next desk over, who has an annoying habit of loudly slurping his coffee.

Step 2: Begin working backward

Try to identify what came immediately before this situation. Imagine that events are like links in a chain, and you are working your way back one link at a time.

What happened before your headache? And before you started to notice your murderous rage for your colleague? Well, you overslept and missed the train. That made you pretty grumpy.

But why did you miss the train? Working almost like a forensic detective, you piece the sequence together: You overslept because you went to bed too late, because you sat up for two hours scrolling social media, because you got a particularly irresistible notification that drew you in. It's a long chain, but your headache and anger at your colleague actually have roots in the night before, in your own behavior.

Step 3: Settle on the "root cause"

Keep going until you feel like you've identified the core reason for the phenomenon you are witnessing in the present. Of course, it's unnecessary to go all the way back to the dawn of mankind and original sin; merely see if you can spot where the crucial sequence of events really kicked off.

You could possibly keep going backward and backward and decide that your own mother was ultimately the cause of all your problems since she gave birth to you . . . but you decide that it's more reasonable to focus on the part of the chain that you actually have agency over: the part where your actions kept you staying up very late at night.

Step 4: Plan

Based on what you've learned, make a plan to take remedial action. The Buddhists will say that it is impossible to go back and change the past; our karma stays with us and must be worked through until we purify and release ourselves. Even still, we can allow ourselves to make better choices right now, in the present, as well as take steps that can mitigate any damage done.

You can't do anything to change your colleague, and you can't go back in time and give yourself a better night's sleep. What you can do is change how you behave today. You also make a list of a few things that might help you get better sleep, be on time for the train, and so on in the future.

Step 5: Take action

One of the best ways to overcome the consequences of a misstep or a poor choice is to take action—not dwell on how bad those consequences are! Take the right action at the right time.

You get home that evening and install a social media blocker on your phone, adjust your notification settings, and make a commitment to keep your phone in another room entirely after 9 p.m.

If you take this action now, it will set off a chain reaction in a completely different direction. You are setting up some "good karma" for yourself. You'll sleep better, wake up on time, get the train on time, and arrive at work feeling far less frazzled and overtired. When you make the tiny decision to change your social media phone behavior, it ultimately allows you to be more productive at work, more relaxed, and more compassionate to your colleagues...

As you can imagine, however, the above process is not infallible. The technique can only be as good as the people employing it, so make allowances for the fact that you don't always have all the necessary information, and that you may be looking at the situation with biases and blind spots.

What's more, we should try to avoid "epistemological arrogance" and assume that we do or even can see all the complex, interconnected causes of the phenomena around us. That said, we are always empowered to do the best we can with what we have in the moment. In fact, that's all any of us *can* do!

Acting Without Acting

"Nature does not rush, yet everything is accomplished."

Lao Tzu

The Daoists have a philosophy called *wu wei*, which translates from the Chinese as "no action."

It can be an incredibly difficult concept to explain, especially for people who have inhabited mental models that emphasize the primacy of conscious, deliberate (even difficult) action. *Wu wei* is not about laziness, passivity, or apathy. Rather, it's pointing to an attitude of *ease*. It speaks of a particular absence of effort . . . and how this can nevertheless achieve so, so much.

In the previous section, we used the lens of karmic cause-and-effect to take a closer look at how all the elements of existence come into being, and how we might in turn use our own agency and awareness to start influencing these processes, or at least undoing the negative influence we've had in the past! While this can certainly be a useful frame, there is another world of possibility if we expand and shift our understanding of "effort" and "action" itself.

Most of us have had a particular worldview drilled into us: no pain no gain. It's a kind of muscular approach to life, where we imagine that getting what we want or bringing about the things we want to bring about is a question of force. We imagine that the world is inert and mechanistic, and that it's up to us to tame it, make it bend to our will, and heroically achieve our goals.

***Wu wei* takes a much gentler view on things. It asks us to imagine how we would proceed if we didn't have these expectations or attachments to particular outcomes**. What would happen if we aligned ourselves—submitted, even—to the already flowing currents of life, rather than strenuously tried to always control that flow? The philosophy of *wu wei* says that something paradoxical happens: We are more effective.

It's not difficult to think of all those things in life that are more difficult the harder we try:

- The more you try to make yourself relax and fall asleep, the less likely you are to do so.
- The more you try to force creativity and insight, the more it eludes you.
- The more you try to deliberately create chemistry or good feeling, the more awkward things feel.

You see, **it's not always true that effort is directly proportional to outcome**. Sometimes people (because of their attachment to particular outcomes, because of their limited vision, because of their lack of wisdom . . . or because of their big fat egos) direct all their efforts in entirely the wrong way. So, *wu wei* is ultimately about harmony.

It's about flowing with nature, rather than exhausting and upsetting yourself in the attempt to always push against it.

- When you do nothing in particular and let go, you find you fall asleep easily and without trying.
- When you play and daydream and let go of any expectations, you find yourself struck by a flash of creativity.
- When you are playful and at ease, and when you least expect it, you find yourself falling in love.

With the philosophy of *wu wei*, you learn to get out of your own way and to get out of the way of the natural flow of things as they already are. Of course, you are awake, you are aware, and you may very well still take action. But you are **less tense, less serious, less ego-filled**. It is as though you accidentally fall into precisely the right outcome, without spending a single atom more energy than you need to. It's effortless!

Wu wei does not mean that you never take any action . . . It does mean that sometimes a lot less action is required than you think. How many times in life have you been deeply upset by something and stressed over what you should do, and yet with a little time, the issue simply resolved itself? Bruce Lee understood the power of *wu wei*, but he saw that it was not about surrender or weakness, but the opposite:

> "Be like water making its way through cracks. Do not be assertive, but adjust to the object, and you shall find a way around or through it. If nothing within you stays rigid, outward things will disclose themselves... Now, water can flow or it can crash. Be water, my friend."

Sometimes, diplomacy, tact, and a gentle touch achieve more than force and domination ever will. Sometimes, the easier path is genuinely the best one. If we believe on some level that struggle, effort, and hard work are the only legitimate ways to accomplish anything, we may not only burn ourselves out, but miss crucial signs along the way that what we are doing is actually not in harmony, either with external nature or with our own internal conscience and intuition.

We barge ahead, trying to be heroic, and fail to realize that 90 percent of our mission is self-imposed, unnecessary, or outright mistaken. How much of our effort in life goes toward making things harder for us than they need to be? *Wu wei* is about learning to be "in the zone," flowing with harmony, and being aligned with forces larger and wiser than ourselves.

So far so good, but how on earth do you apply such a life philosophy?

The first thing is, naturally, that applying *wu wei* should feel effortless! There is no point getting yourself tangled in a web of expectation, doubt, struggle, and a list of serious demands on yourself or reality. This is not about meritocracy or being "good" enough or finding some secret magical enlightenment moment that acts like a cheat code for life.

Instead, imagine that this mental model is more like an attitude, an approach, or a feeling. It's not something you do, but a *way* you do it. It's a mood.

Here are a few things to contemplate and questions to ask yourself when faced with a situation in which you're tempted to dive in and take strenuous action to "fix" things.

How would this be different if everything was easy?

It may be that your own unreasonable expectations (clue words: should, must, have to) or sense of perfectionism are creating the sense that things are more serious than they are. Use Occam's razor, too, to ask if you may be unintentionally complicating things for yourself. There are always many, many possibilities and options to move forward . . . and there is always the option to do nothing.

Maria, for example, frequently falls into the trap of assuming that everything is her responsibility, and that others will automatically judge and condemn her for not taking charge and making everything run seamlessly.

But when she asks herself how her approach would differ if things were *easy*, she starts to see that she is not in fact the only one responsible. She sees that the world is very capable of running along without her! When she takes a step back, she realizes that *it's okay for things to be easy*, and that she doesn't need to chase drama or difficulty in order to feel needed or important. Rather, she can sit back sometimes and let things unfold. Very often, she can't even remember what she was so worried about in the first place.

How much effort is really appropriate here?

Our sporting heroes always say that they give 110 percent, and there isn't anything wrong with that. It is always a possibility that we do more, go further, and push ourselves. While this can bring results, it can also backfire, burn us out, or sap our joy.

For small, easy tasks, apply only a little energy. For more difficult ones, start small and gradually ramp up your effort to match the situation—but not exceed it. There's nothing wrong with pulling back when you notice that you're really straining. Take a rest, regroup, and try again a little later. Difficult things can be done without burning ourselves out. Just imagine Bruce Lee's water and how it can wear away solid rock simply by being what it is and flowing.

Your "flow state" will *never* be one where you are exhausted, straining, and overwhelmed. It will be in that sweet spot between too easy and too hard. Kelvin learned this skill the hard way; as a marathon runner, he knew that in the long run (pun intended!), he was a more effective runner and healthier human when he could pace himself and dial back sometimes, rather than always pushing himself to do more and more.

Are you making unrealistic demands?

So much of the stuff we believe we "should" be doing comes not from reality itself but from our own expectations and belief systems about what reality means and where our place is relative to it. But a very strong desire for things to be different than they are is a mindset that can only bring distress and exhaustion.

Isn't it strange how often we simply assume that our wants, our desires, and our expectations are sound, and automatically get angry at life for not accommodating them? Yet most of us can picture a time in our past (remember being a teenager?) where our demands were incredibly narrow and based on our own very limited understanding of the world. Why should that not be the case now, too?

The next time you believe yourself to be facing a problem, ask yourself if it really is one . . . or whether the problem is a function of your perspective, your expectations, or a demand you're making on yourself, others, or reality. Why do we hold on so tightly to our preconceived ideas about how things should go? Why do we think that all our judgments are correct, and that we always know best? Why do we force things, often for no other reason than that we feel life should conform to the orders of our ego, rather than someone else's?

Beth had a major epiphany when she considered this question. When faced with the problem of her failing marriage, she realized she had dozens of demands and expectations. What's more, she felt ashamed that she was having trouble in the first place. While she still did what she could to save the marriage, she also realized that it was useless to beat herself up for being in the situation. Ironically, Beth had the inflexible belief "My marriage should be easy," and this led to struggle. It was only when she let go of this demand that she was able to bring more genuine ease to the situation. Was it really true that marriages should always be easy?

Can you be in the situation, right now, as it is?

Often, what we perceive as problem-solving behavior is merely avoidance—we want to run away from discomfort as quickly as possible. But having this attitude makes us reactive, fearful, unconscious. It actually makes us worse problem-solvers!

Instead, a bit of mindfulness can help us remain in the moment and experience it fully, without resistance, without clinging, and without interpretation. Sometimes, to our surprise, we realize that strong negative feelings simply come and go. If we had gotten entangled in that feeling as it emerged, we would have set off a chain of events, a string of action and consequence, that might never have needed to happen if we merely waited and watched that impulse float away again.

Jessica has learned to find moments of mindfulness any time she is faced with a big decision or any time she feels unsettled or disturbed by something. She knows that if she can just stop, take a step back, breathe, and be in the moment, she can calm down and take a more balanced look at the situation and her own reactions. This self-awareness brings her so much more ease. She notices, for example, that when she gets intense cravings to indulge in a bad habit, she simply stops and becomes curious.

She just "sits with" the feeling. She "rides it out." And every single time, she notices that within a few minutes, the urge that once felt so important and irresistible simply fades away. In other words, many of our problems are problems we make for ourselves whenever we react habitually to fleeting stimuli. If we just keep still, disengage, and become aware, we teach ourselves that not every stimulus needs to be acted on, and no stimulus lasts forever. In fact, just because something is demanding your attention, it doesn't mean you have to give it!

Chesterton's Fence

"Rage and frenzy will pull down more in half an hour than prudence, deliberation, and foresight can build up in a hundred years."

Edmund Burke

Imagine one day a well-meaning man (read: a bit of a busybody) is walking around in the fields and sees a fence. It's an old fence, and he's not exactly sure who built it or why. The fence is ancient and so rotten it's nearly crumbling away . . . not to mention it's a nuisance to climb over.

He looks around and sees nothing but cows contentedly grazing in the surrounding fields. Clearly, the fence has no purpose. Knowing that many walkers come through this area, and realizing that he himself is inconvenienced by the ugly old fence, he decides to "help" by kicking it down. It's clearly an old thing that no longer serves its purpose anyway, he thinks.

Fast forward a few months, and all the cows in the field are dead. The fence, as old and rotten as it was, had acted to keep out badgers who sometimes carry deadly tuberculosis strains, as well as sheep who might come in and eat the grass to the very root, leaving the cows, who needed to eat longer grass, to starve.

This is the story put forward by G.K. Chesterton in his book *The Thing: Why I am a Catholic*. The analogy illustrates how well-intentioned reformers can unwittingly cause trouble in their attempt to modernize, update, and "help." In the story, the harm comes not from evil intentions, but something more like a lack of imagination, a too-narrow understanding, or a simple deficiency of understanding of the bigger picture. A poor decision was made because someone wrongly assumed, "This thing serves no purpose," when in fact it did.

Chesterton used this line of reasoning to caution us against jumping on bandwagons where the goal is to helpfully remake the past, kick down old conventions and rules, and merrily assume that the solutions erected by our ancestors don't apply to us anymore.

A slightly different take on the tale: A meddling man sees a fence in the field and declares, "It's useless. We can take it down." An older, wiser farmer advises him, "The fence is there to keep out the wolves." The meddling man looks around and sees no wolves. In fact, there haven't been wolves in this area for decades. "Not only is this fence useless, but this old man and his outdated ideas are just as useless," he thinks to himself. He kicks the fence down and discovers the awful truth: The reason there were no wolves to be seen is that the fence was keeping them at bay.

Chesterton was pointing to larger, societal "fences" and the implications of removing them. He saw certain cultural artifacts as necessary—even if we didn't always see who had put them up or understand exactly why they were there. Philosopher Edmund Burke came to a similar conclusion: **Gradual reform is always preferable to sudden, drastic change that may have unexpected consequences.**

This idea is not just for bigger-picture ideas, but can be used in our own everyday lives. It's important to realize, also, that Chesterton is not suggesting that everything old and established is right, and nobody should ever attempt any "reform." Rather, he says:

> "The more intelligent type of reformer [who] will do well to say: 'If you don't see the use of it, I certainly won't let you clear it away. Go away and think. Then, when you can come back and tell me that you do see the use of it, I may allow you to destroy it.'"

Therefore, the point is not old versus new, but rather understanding versus a lack of understanding. **If you wish to make big changes and important decisions, then the onus is on you to make sure that you really, truly *understand* what you're doing, why, and what the likely consequences are to be**. The trick, of course, is that the factors that Chesterton warns us about are precisely those which we are least likely to be aware of!

This mental model, then, is a meta-mental model, since it forces us to think carefully about our conceptualization—is the way we conceive of a problem really the wisest and best evidenced?

Think of it as an extension of the karma concept—every action has a consequence that we must bear, but we should not make the mistake of thinking that we are always perfect actors with full and accurate understanding about the systems we are part of. In fact, the reason *wu wei* may sometimes work in our favor is because we don't see all the relevant causes, effects, and flows of influence—it is when we remove our own foolish understanding of how things should be that our assumptions are shown to be limited.

It may not always be possible to foresee every likely outcome, or to accurately identify your current gaps of understanding. But the concept of Chesterton's fence can encourage you to be more open-minded (and a little humbler) when making big-picture decisions or solving "problems." Here are a few points to ponder that can help you rethink all those things you might currently be framing as outdated or pointless:

Question 1: Is this a type 1 or type 2 decision?

Jeff Bezos introduced the idea of two main types of decisions in his 2015 letter to shareholders. Type 1 decisions, he said, are irreversible or near enough. Tearing down a fence, sentencing someone to the electric chair, taking a potent medicine, permanently severing a relationship, having an arm amputated, or destroying a piece of ancient artwork... all of these are actions that naturally should give us pause.

Bezos claims that any decision with irreversible consequences should be attempted very slowly and with much deliberation (i.e., Chesterton's advice to "go away and think"). You need to keep in mind all the *negative* outcomes and let these guide you.

Type 2 decisions, on the other hand, have reversible consequences. They may be easy to undo or quite challenging, but you *can* come back from the changes you introduce. These, Bezos says, require a different mindset. Here, you need to weigh up the pros and cons, but you can give considerably more weight to potential benefits and start to view the decision in terms of the *positive* outcomes it might bring. This will orient you to stay curious and open-minded and take a scientist's approach to the matter at hand.

Decide which kind of decision you are looking at. If you are too rash and excitable about a Type 1 decision, you could end up with irreversible consequences (and more problems), but if you are too slow and cautious with a Type 2 decision, you could incur opportunity costs and waste time when you could be gathering data and learning from mistakes.

Question 2: WHY are things currently the way they are?

When you are in problem-solving mode, it's easy to slip into the attitude that the current status is simply wrong, and the only desired outcome is to bring it more in line with what you think is right—i.e., to make the situation into what you personally want. But there is a subtle trap here: Merely changing things in the world to suit your preference is not automatically the same thing as "solving problems."

If you are too focused on the outcome you're trying to bring about, then you may miss out on crucial information—i.e., what is currently unfolding right in front of you. This means you don't truly understand what you're dealing with.

Let's say you are hired to boost productivity in an office, and you come in and immediately start trying to identify areas of waste or mismanagement. You notice that the sales team is spending enormous amounts of money every month taking prospective clients out for fancy dinners. You clamp down on this spending and save the company money . . . but in six months sales have dropped to a third of their normal volume.

Why? In retrospect you can see that the fancy dinners, although expensive, were actually creating more revenue in the long run. Because you didn't fully understand the role of these dinners in the broader company culture, you removed that "fence" and saw that actually, customer relations depended heavily on the kind of hospitality and network-building that seemed at first glance to be wasteful.

In looking at your own big decisions and problems in life, take a close look at all those elements you suppose are useless or unnecessary, and instead become curious about how they fit into the system. Start from the assumption that everything, even a really annoying or outdated rule, *is there for a reason* and serves a purpose.

Fences don't grow by themselves from the ground, and people don't decide one morning to build a fence for no reason at all. In the same way, everything around you now came to be because of a series of choices and decisions in the past. What were they?

Question 3: What are your real reasons for wanting to act?

In his essay collection, *Heretics*, Chesterton gives another story:

> "Suppose that a great commotion arises in the street about something, let us say a lamp-post, which many influential persons desire to pull down. A grey-clad monk, who is the spirit of the Middle Ages, is approached upon the

matter, and begins to say, in the arid manner of the Schoolmen, "Let us first of all consider, my brethren, the value of Light. If Light be in itself good—" At this point he is somewhat excusably knocked down. All the people make a rush for the lamp-post, the lamp-post is down in ten minutes, and they go about congratulating each other on their unmediaeval practicality. But as things go on they do not work out so easily. Some people have pulled the lamp-post down because they wanted the electric light; some because they wanted old iron; some because they wanted darkness, because their deeds were evil. Some thought it not enough of a lamp-post, some too much; some acted because they wanted to smash municipal machinery; some because they wanted to smash something. And there is war in the night, no man knowing whom he strikes. So, gradually and inevitably, to-day, to-morrow, or the next day, there comes back the conviction that the monk was right after all, and that all depends on what is the philosophy of Light. Only what we might have discussed under the gas-lamp, we now must discuss in the dark."

Now, Chesterton is a Christian apologist, and his point here is a cultural and theological one. He is alluding to the eternal tension between conserving the tradition and wisdom of the past, and the urge to break away from that past, rebel, innovate, and progress to something believed to be better.

But the principle also has more practical applications in our everyday lives. How often do we simply revert to the assumption that everyone in the past was a pitiable fool, and all their ideas quaint but best forgotten? How often do we discount the thousands of years of experience and wisdom that came before us and assume that the only worthwhile things that have happened to humanity just so happened to occur in the last decade or two?

In the same way, how often does our urge to change, improve, and fix our lives mean we conveniently forget the past and ignore the advice and wisdom that comes from those older than us—or even from previous versions of ourselves in the past? Sometimes, the urge to improve/renovate/upgrade also comes with a kind of historical blindness. This blindness means we miss out on a world of potentially valuable information.

Be very, very honest about why you want to change something. Is it really because the current state of affairs is outdated, backward, foolish, useless? Or might it be because of your own ego? In Chesterton's lamp story, not everyone who tears down the lamp is doing so for noble, revolutionary reasons. In the same way, not everyone who motivates for a big change is doing so for a valid reason.

If we are honest, some of the big decisions in our lives come with a host of official reasons... while the real motivation is kept secret, sometimes even from ourselves. A little humility can make us pause and find this honesty. We may arrogantly pronounce that something needs to change, and that our vision for the future is the right one, but Chesterton reminds us that often, our understanding of "improvement" can very easily be tainted by our own fear, arrogance, or greed.

Hilary is a proud animal rights activist and decides the right thing to do would be to become a vegan. She is already a vegetarian but decides to further cut out all dairy and eggs. Unfortunately, cutting these foods out leaves her so hungry and unsatisfied that she finds that within a few months, she is repeatedly binging on fatty fast food—

including meat. While she had managed to be a healthy and consistent vegetarian for many years, her vegan diet fails within just a few months, and she finds herself eating in a way that deeply violates her own principles.

She is utterly disgusted with herself, but soon realizes the irony in her quest to be better: The eggs and dairy were precisely the "bad habits" that were allowing her to be such a good and consistent vegetarian in the first place! It made sense that cutting out eggs and dairy was the "right thing to do" in the short term . . . but in the long term it actually resulted in a worse outcome. The dairy and eggs were a "fence" that at first appeared to be getting in her way, but on closer reflection they acted as a kind of useful barrier.

Hilary didn't understand that her "bad habit" actually served a function. As much as she hated to admit it, the dietary wisdom held by every generation before her was fairly sound—eat a moderate and balanced diet with a little of everything in it. After adjusting her diet once more, Hilary realizes that part of her reason for wanting to be a vegan was not what she originally claimed it was. Rather, her own ego's desire to "be good" and ideologically pure had taken over.

Summary

- Karma is a principle describing how actions emerge from thoughts and feelings, and how those actions then create our world through the power of cause and effect. Everything in this world that exists right now came into being because of a particular cause. Virtuous acts bring about harmony; unvirtuous ones bring about suffering and confusion.
- We can understand all our actions as resulting from the interaction between our karmic urge and the environmental conditions we face. Conscious humans can act to resist their karmic habits and momentum. Be aware of the consequences of every choice you make and the greater karmic and moral implications of what you do, think, and say.
- Karma can also help us solve problems by understanding the root cause behind the consequences we see in our lives.
- The concept of *wu wei* is "action without action" and finding a way to flow with the harmony of nature. The paradox is that if we proceed without expectations or attachments to particular outcomes, we tend to be more effective. Be less tense, serious, and ego-filled, and realize that

sometimes less effort is required than we think.
- The analogy of Chesterton's fence tells us that gradual reform was always preferable to sudden, drastic change that may have unexpected consequences. We should not remove things that we don't properly understand the function of. If you wish to make big changes and important decisions, make sure that you truly understand the likely consequences.
- Check if something is a Type 1 (irreversible) or Type 2 (reversible) decision, be honest about your motivations, and try to understand the function of things you consider problematic or useless.

Chapter 3: Meaning and Long-Term Decision-Making

Let's once more turn the "objective lens" on our theoretical microscope and take a look at the problems and decisions of life in yet another way. It's one thing to ponder over the smaller choices: what to have for breakfast, which Netflix show to watch, whether to take your umbrella to work or leave it at home.

As we zoom out, however, we start to see the finer details of logic, rationality, and cause-and-effect dissolve, and a bigger picture comes into focus. In the long term, how do all these details add up to create a life? What do we see if we stop considering the individual brushstrokes of the painting of our life and take a step back to see the overall picture? What is the scene we have created? Is it in proportion? Does it all hang together? Is it *beautiful*?

In this section, we take a more abstract and philosophical look at choice, free will, and the unfolding of our lives. We will consider the work of Nietzsche, Pascal, and the Zen Buddhists.

Nietzschean Eternal Recurrence

"My doctrine says: the task is to live in such a way that you must wish to live again—you will anyway!"

Nietzsche

Let's get one thing straight: The work of philosopher Frederik Nietzsche has always been difficult to interpret, even by (or perhaps most by) other philosophers. Nietzsche was a nihilist, which meant that he thought that all values were unfounded, that life essentially lacked meaning, and that nothing in life could really be known or communicated. Whereas most people would see this stance as a little depressing, Nietzsche seems to argue that it instead poses an exhilarating potential for human freedom—in fact, the only real hope is in embracing this meaninglessness.

If life really is meaningless and no values or decisions are better or worse than any others, how on earth can we conduct ourselves? Nietzsche's mental model here is the doctrine of the eternal recurrence. **The idea is that whatever you choose for yourself, you should try to imagine what it would be like to make that decision over and over again eternally.** Think of it as a "Type 0" decision—not only is the consequence irreversible and permanent, but it repeats in a loop forever.

It's a strange concept, but Nietzsche clearly intended for it to help us discern a particular quality behind our choices that went beyond them being practical, conventional, convenient, or morally good. Nietzsche advises us to never act in a way where we hold in the back of our minds the hope that we can always change our minds later. Rather, we should choose in a way that we will be willing to endure the consequences forever.

It's arguable whether the philosopher thought that life actually was this way, or merely that it might be helpful to imagine it did as a kind of thought experiment. Some have suggested (Nadeem Hussain, for example) that the exercise is one that helps us reframe the meaninglessness of life and actually live in hope and freedom.

In this section, we're not going to get carried away with a deeper philosophical examination of Nietzsche's ideas. Rather, we'll see if his overall mental model can be adapted to our own ends. If you're facing a major life decision, but moral or practical approaches are not helping you gain any clarity, consider the following points.

Desire

Think about what you actually want, "beyond good and evil."

Nietzsche believed that moral judgments are usually just personal preferences in disguise, and that there really is no such thing as right and wrong. Regardless of whether you agree or not, it's worth taking a closer look at how you're thinking about your decisions in these terms. The nihilist would say that whenever we make a pronouncement that something is good or bad, we are really just expressing an opinion or some kind of inherited cultural habit—we are not actually making a valid claim about reality.

But sometimes, labeling something "good" or "bad" can have the effect of halting our critical thinking in that area. We assume that we want good things and not bad things. But can we turn this around and use the question of eternal recurrence to ask, "Whether it's labeled good or bad, what do I actually want for myself? What do I want enough that I could imagine doing it forever?"

Jenny, for example, has always assumed that her life path is to be a doctor. Both her parents were doctors, her culture tells her that this job is a noble and valuable one (as does the salary), and she has never questioned the idea that being a helper and a healer is a "good" thing.

But once Jenny qualifies and starts practicing as a doctor, she realizes that she doesn't really *want* to be. She can't picture doing that career for another year, let alone the rest of her life or eternity. Had she probed a little deeper into what she thought was "good," she might have seen sooner that the onus was on her to create her own meaning and value, rather than merely assume the one given to her was adequate.

Ultimately, nihilism is probably an unworkable life philosophy. Nevertheless, we can uncover some interesting insights if we strip away all the usual yardsticks of meaning and dig deep within—if we and only we were forced to endure the consequences of our choices for the rest of eternity, would we still make the choice?

Consequence

Think about long-term consequences . . . *really* long term.

Take a step back. Set aside your current feelings and wishes about the decision at hand and take a broader view; one broad enough to see the unfolding of your entire life. Imagine that a particular decision will repeat itself all throughout the rest of time . . . In a way, it will, because there will be consequences to that choice, and consequences to those consequences, and so on.

What you choose will create the person you are in the future, and that person will make their own choices. Do you choose *that*?

The teenager who gets a tattoo has made a choice in the moment, but the marks on his skin are likely to remain there long after the attitude that brought them about fades and changes over time. In the teenager's mind, a lion with flames for a mane emblazoned on his chest sounds like a fantastic idea. But will it always be a fantastic idea? A teenager will eventually become a young adult, then a middle-aged one, and maybe eventually an elderly one.

When the teenager chose to get the tattoo, in effect he did continue to make that decision for the rest of his life. Every day he wakes up, it will be as if he consents once more to have that tattoo on his chest.

When we have regrets, we look back and say, "I wish I had thought differently then. I wish I had known how I would feel in the future." Perhaps Nietzsche is asking us to perform the reverse function: "If I look forward and see all of my life unfolding in the future, might I think differently now? Might I make a different choice?"

Acceptance

Think about embracing your life as it actually is, right now.

In *The Gay Science*, Nietzsche offers a story that illustrates his idea of eternal recurrence:

> "What if some day or night a demon were to steal into your loneliest loneliness and say to you: 'This life as you now live and have lived it you will have to live once again and innumerable times again; and there will be nothing new in it, but every pain and every joy and every thought and sigh and everything unspeakably small or great in your life must return to you, all in the same succession and sequence— even this spider and this moonlight

between the trees, and even this moment and I myself. The eternal hourglass of existence is turned upside down again and again, and you with it, speck of dust!'"

He continues:

"The question in each and every thing, 'Do you want this again and innumerable times again?' would lie on your actions as the heaviest weight! Or how well disposed would you have to become to yourself and to life to long for nothing more fervently than for this ultimate eternal confirmation and seal?"

Many of us make decisions on the assumption that the future is a place of endless unfolding possibility, of things forever being different from what they are now. In fact, many of us have almost put our current lives on hold for this imagined future, saying to ourselves things like, "Once I graduate, things will be better," or, "Just as soon as I find a better job, I'll be more relaxed," and so on. But what if there is no "Just as soon as . . ."? What if there is no heaven and hell waiting for us, but only this moment right now?

Nietzsche's story prompts us to take a completely different view on life. What would it take for us to accept and affirm—even rejoice in—our life? In all its imperfection and smallness? One way to interpret Nietzsche's provocations is a little in line with what the ancient Greeks called *amor fati*, or love of one's fate. If there wasn't anyone coming to save us, and there was no impressive "after" picture where all the problems that bug us currently have disappeared, could we bravely and honestly embrace our life just as it is?

If not, the exercise can still point us in a useful direction. Can we choose those actions—or even those states of mind—that we would be happy to choose again? What brings you so much meaning that you would happily embrace it forever, with no improvement and no addition? What kind of Groundhog Day could you accept?

Nietzsche goes on to say,

> "I want to learn more and more to see as beautiful what is necessary in things; then I shall be one of those who make things beautiful. Amor fati [love of fate]: let that be my love henceforth! I do not want to wage war against what is ugly. I do not want to accuse; I do not even want to accuse those who accuse. Looking away shall be my only negation. And all in all and on the

whole: someday I wish to be only a Yes-sayer."

What might it look like to say *yes* to all of our life, even those parts we are still so anxiously working at fixing? What would it look like to say yes to our own confusion, our mistakes, and our ignorance? If our whole lives were a novel or movie, could we accept the bad with the good and see all of it as necessary and part of the whole?

Again, this is a very strange concept, but it helps illuminate those places where we might act with the assumption that our life is always something we can escape, just something we can temporarily endure for now while we wait for something better, something more real to come along. But what if it never does? What if all we ever have is this day, right now, exactly as it is?

Whatever springs up in you in response to this question is likely to be concerned with meaning and value—*your* sense of meaning and value. Does the thought of the same life forever fill you with dread and fear? Boredom? Tenderness? A kind of peace and acceptance? Whatever answer you give, become curious about what it means for the decisions you're making right now and how you're making them.

Pascal's Wager

"There would be too great a darkness, if truth had not visible signs."

Blaise Pascal

Blaise Pascal was a seventeenth-century French philosopher who came to the conclusion that people ought to believe in God more as less *just in case*.

His argument was that **if God does exist and you believe in him, then you'll live your life in such a way as to be rewarded in the afterlife. However, if you don't believe in God, and he does exist, then you will likely end up living in a way that earns you eternal damnation.**

If, however, you chose to believe in God and conduct yourself accordingly, and it turned out that there was no God after all, then the worst you've done is live a good life and believe in something that turned out not to be true.

Basically, Pascal looked at it all with a gambler's perspective: Believing "cost" you nothing or very little, but if your bet turned out to be right, the reward would be great. We can plot out Pascal's variables like this:

	God Exists	God Does Not Exist
Believe in God	Eternal Happiness	Nothing
Do Not Believe	Eternal Misery	Nothing

From Pascal's point of view, there are only a very few possibilities here; in fact, there are exactly four. Looking at the table above, it probably strikes you that there are two neutral outcomes, one great outcome, and one awful one. Given this, or so says Pascal, we may as well take the (cheap) gamble that God does exist, and hedge our bets, so to speak.

Now, many people from different walks of life have found Pascal's wager a little ridiculous, for various reasons. Christopher Hitchens called the argument "hucksterism" since he considered it a flimsy trick to dupe people into believing. Others (namely, believers) point out that Pascal obviously had a very limited understanding of faith and the nature of belief, God, and the afterlife.

There are problems with Pascal's argument in that he forces a black-or-white decision where it isn't clear there needs to be one (believe or don't believe), and he simplifies quite a complex matter to a ridiculous degree, probably removing in the process the more subtle and important features.

But the appropriateness of this line of reasoning for the topic at hand (i.e., whether or not to believe in God) is actually the least interesting thing about Pascal's wager. We can still use the logic and principle behind his argument because its key mechanism—namely, pointing to **asymmetric payoffs**—is essential to understand when it comes to prudent decision-making.

The gambler/mathematician/logician will say that in life, the outcomes of certain decisions and choices are seldom equal or symmetrical. Some choices cost a lot and yield little; some cost nothing at all, but if they "pay off," they bring enormous rewards; and some are either so unpredictable or cost so little to buy into that you may as well do so on the off chance that things work in your favor.

How might the mental model behind Pascal's wager work in our more everyday lives?

Let's consider a decision you may have had to make in your life at some point: the choice between the guaranteed old and the potentially-good-but-still-unknown new. For example, you always take a week's vacation to Spot A every year, and you do so because you like it there and you're familiar with the routine of going there. It's pretty much a guaranteed good time.

But one day you consider taking your vacation in Spot B. This location could very well be a perfect spot—possibly even better than Spot A—but there is a non-zero chance that you end up hating it, not to mention losing a week of vacation time and a bunch of money in the process.

What would you do? What is the rational thing to do?

Let's map the choices out just as Pascal did. You have a single decision to make between two options, and this yields four possible outcomes:

Outcome 1: Spot B is perfect and you choose Spot B—EXCELLENT

Outcome 2: Spot B is perfect and you don't choose it, but default to Spot A—FINE

Outcome 3: Spot B is horrible and you choose Spot B—BAD

Outcome 4: Spot B is horrible and you don't choose it, but default to Spot A—FINE

But the outcome is not all we have to worry about here. Looking at the above list, it's clear that Outcome 1 would be preferable, followed by either Outcome 2 or Outcome 4. The only way we can learn which is the best outcome, however, is to choose and see what happens.

But choosing costs us—so, let's ask which choice costs the most. Choosing Spot B can either lead to a BAD or EXCELLENT outcome, whereas choosing Spot A as usual always leads to a FINE outcome. Doesn't that mean we should just choose Spot A, since it's guaranteed?

Well, here is where Pascal's wager can help us tease our decisions apart with a little more care and really understand the costs and rewards of the decisions we make and the assumptions that go with those decisions. Because there is also a cost to choosing Spot A—if we choose Spot A when Spot B was the better place all along, then the cost we have paid is the cost of losing that potentially great vacation. **This is an opportunity cost, and it's often invisible to us when making decisions of this kind.**

Choosing in such a way as to maximize stability and predictability feels like the most logical thing in the world, but all the while we may be accruing invisible losses in the form of better experiences we unwittingly passed up.

Pascal's wager teaches us two important concepts: that of the **forced bet**, and, as already mentioned, **asymmetric payoffs**. By forcing your hand between one of two choices, you are pushing yourself to realize that by opting for one thing, you are actively NOT opting for another. Many of us make decisions that are essentially a choice between maintaining the status quo over taking a gamble on a potential massive payoff. While Pascal's wager may seem too simplistic, this is a part of its value—it forces you to whittle down your decisions to the bare bones and see exactly what you're dealing with in terms of costs and benefits.

The next time you're making a big decision, see how the factors fit into a decision-matrix like the one Pascal set up. Purposefully measure up both the cost and the benefit of *not* acting. Look at opportunity costs—you may gain something by making a choice (certainty, predictability), but might there be something better you're giving up (i.e., the chance for something much better than certainty)? How big is that chance? If there is only a teeny-tiny chance of a big payoff, but the cost to find out is small, might it be worth making that decision anyway? The easiest choice to make in any moment might be to simply carry on as you are . . . but what do you lose by doing so? Not just now but far into the future?

Understanding Risk, Value, and Decision-Making as a "Bet"

Nina has a great idea for a business and has dreamed for a long time of making it the primary source of income for her family. Just as she's gearing up to go into business for herself, however, she receives an offer to work a more conventional job for a company that will bring more stability, structure, and certainty. On offer is a satisfactory salary every month and a few nice perks.

Here's Nina's choice: Does she go it alone and start her own business, or does she take the sure-thing job offer and work the conventional job instead?

On the one hand, financial security for her loved ones means a great deal to her, and it would be fantastic not to have to worry about money. On the other, she doesn't particularly enjoy the work and can already see herself becoming bored with it, especially as it would mean giving up her dream to be her own boss. On the *other* hand (how many hands are we up to already?), striking out on her own may be exciting and could earn her plenty of money, but it also carries with it enormous risks.

The first thing Nina realizes is that she needs to look at the problem from many different angles. Her feelings and emotions are important, but she decides to set those aside for a moment and instead look at the matter as coolly as possible. How can she be strategic and calculating in how she weighs up all the separate factors of risk, cost, benefit, and uncertainty?

She draws up a table much like the ones we saw earlier and realizes a few interesting things:

- The "sure thing" job may be relatively more certain, but it's not actually *100 percent certain*. After all, the company may go under, or her pay may be cut. Anything could happen, and she would not necessarily be in control of it.
- At the same time, it's not a 100 percent certainty that her own business will fail.
- Looking at the costs incurred with each choice, she realizes that choosing the conventional job is not the easy, safe choice she first thought. Factoring in opportunity costs, she realizes that the security of that monthly check comes at quite a high price—she will have to give up on her dream (maybe forever?) as well as potentially lose out on her chance to do so in the future (her business idea may not be as viable in five years' time, she may not be as energetic or motivated, etc.).

- There may be other costs to choosing the conventional job, beyond opportunity costs—for example, an additional commute or a loss of freedom.

So which decision should Nina make?

Well, that's not so easy to say. Nina herself needs to weigh these things up against her own goals and values and decide where her personal threshold for risk is. **But what she undoubtedly should do is choose the option where the favorable outcomes are larger than the unfavorable ones.**

Pascal's wager helps us make decisions even when we are not entirely clear about the probabilities of outcomes. Instead, we can **focus on the size of the potential payoff.** Where it concerns God, the size of eternal bliss in heaven is so big that you should choose to believe in God. For Nina, the size of the benefit of succeeding at her own business is so large that she should choose to take on that risk.

This may seem very counterintuitive, but the fact is, few of us know with certainty what the probabilities of every outcome are (what are Nina's chances of succeeding as an entrepreneur? Or of being fired from her new job? Nobody really knows. It's all conjecture). We can, however, measure up the size of a potential benefit. If Nina could make her new business a success, it would completely and utterly change her life. That's quite a big payoff! The corollary is that passing that up is quite a large price to pay.

Nina considers things very carefully and decides that the best possible outcome of the conventional job is not as good as the best possible outcome of starting her own business. If both of them incur costs and lost opportunities, she decides she'd rather "bet" on the option that, should it work, will bring truly great rewards.

You may be wondering, "What if Nina's new business fails?"

Well, this is a possibility. But in thinking of things in such terms, Nina also allows herself to make contingency plans, to prepare, and to take *deliberate, calculated risks*. She doesn't know how likely it is that she will succeed, but she can do everything in her power to mitigate all the potential threats she can predict will come her way.

Nina's decision may seem a little rash to others, but that's only because she is factoring in certain variables that others may be ignoring. If you've ever felt that your life was kind of mediocre, that it passed you by, or that you had maybe played things too small, you may already have a faint inkling of the real costs that Nina's choice was designed to avoid.

Try to remember:

- Consequences matter more than probabilities.
- When you choose something, there is something else that you necessarily give up.
- There is no such thing as not choosing—inaction is a choice and also comes with costs.

A great strategy is to look at the options in front of you and decide to choose the one that will cost you the least but bring the biggest rewards—regardless of how probable each outcome is. Once you've made that decision, then become curious about what you can do to mitigate potential problems and increase the chances of the best outcome happening. Playing it safe *might* be the best way forward sometimes . . . but confirm for yourself that this is truly the case, rather than merely choosing the status quo out of fear, uncertainty, intolerance, or laziness.

Adopting a Beginner's Mind

"In the beginner's mind there are many possibilities, but in the expert's there are few."

Shunryo Suzuki

Let's stay with Nina and the difficult choice she has to make. Let's imagine that Nina grew up in a working-class family that always struggled for money, and that her mother always stressed the value of supporting your family no matter what. Let's say that Nina also grew up in a particular era that strongly valued "independent women" who worked hard, made their own fortune, and challenged themselves to rise to their greatest ambitions. Nina's mother thinks it's the responsible and mature thing to do to choose a boring but dependable job and get on with it. She says, "You can't go chasing your dreams when you have a family to worry about!"

Nina's husband disagrees and thinks that she should "go for it" and be brave. He believes in her, he says. She should reach for her dreams, be the best she can be, and ignore anyone who can't recognize how important that is.

But then there is also Nina's close circle of friends, none of whom have high-powered careers. They're all happy for her either way, but the consensus there is that work is something of a necessary evil—why would Nina voluntarily choose all the stress of launching a business when she could spend more quality time with her family, relax, and enjoy the more meaningful things in life? Why not just enjoy the thing as a hobby rather than try to make a big business out of it? Besides, they think, Nina's almost fifty—she's worked all her life. Isn't it time she started enjoying herself a little?

Three different perspectives, all of them valid.

In the previous sections, we've spoken about decisions and choices as though they happened in a vacuum—mere mathematical or probabilistic games that we have only to understand and optimize. But in Nina's case (and probably in your own life, too), it's likely clear that things are never this simple. Nina is not arriving at this decision in a neutral way. Rather, she comes to it with a host of preconceived notions, beliefs, biases, and blind spots—some of them her own, and some of them inherited from others.

Is starting your own business selfish and stupid? Is it a sign of self-respect and courage? Is it a privilege or a boring chore? The more

Nina thinks it over, the more she realizes that she needs to approach the problem with a clear mind, or what the Zen Buddhists would call *shoshin*, "beginner's mind."

Most of us like to think that we are open minded, but are we really? **When you are a "beginner," you take absolutely nothing for granted. You are driven purely by curiosity**, and your position is one of not knowing. It is as though you are discovering something for the first time. But as each of us grows older and more experienced, that experience crystallizes as knowledge, as things we "know." Our minds close and we start to look at the world not as it is, but as we think it is, according to the estimations we made about it a long time ago.

You say, "I know what this is. I've seen this before," and that attitude is precisely what stops you from seeing.

Each of us carries with us a world of entrenched habits and beliefs, as well as ideas and assumptions that come from our family, historical period, and culture. These habits act as a kind of cognitive shorthand and save us the processing power of having to think things over from scratch every second of the day... but they also mean we are no longer quite "learning" in the way we used to. To become experts, we lose the magic of being beginners.

Nina, for example, "knows" that being your own boss is an admirable and awesome thing. She "knows" that the most important thing in life is to go for your dreams, no matter what. But where does this expertise really come from?

The problem with using prior knowledge to guide current decision-making is that we can become lazy over time and forget that this is what we are doing. We may feel as though we are neutral, objective agents making rational decisions, when really, we are just acting to confirm the preconceived ideas we already have and picking those bits of reality that align best with our way of thinking.

When we are making big, important life decisions, this becomes even more important, since the criteria for judging the success of these decisions is often quite personal and subjective—i.e., it's based on meaning. This means it's crucial to really understand how you are making that meaning, what information you are taking in, and what conclusions you're coming to. Occam's razor asked us to choose an explanation with the fewest assumptions. If we adopt a beginner's mind, we do the same, except our focus is on our own beliefs, knowledge, values, and judgments.

Nina decides to set aside all the opinions of the people around her, and what's more, she decides to set aside her own assumptions and preconceived ideas about what a good life is, or what an accomplished and fulfilled woman ought to do with herself. Instead, she tries to clear her mind and **look at the situation not as a wise expert, but as someone who knows absolutely nothing. No preconceptions, no foregone conclusions, no prejudices either way.**

Shoshin is a rich and complex philosophical concept, but we can extract and distill a few small lessons from this mental model and apply them to our own decision-making behavior:

Lesson 1: Don't be in too much of a hurry to fix, label, or arrive at an opinion.

Many of us have been taught that there is something mildly shameful about saying, "I don't know." But there is a lot to be learned about remaining, without struggle, in that state of uncertainty or ignorance. It's certainly better than forcing a premature conclusion just to convince yourself that you are in control!

You don't need to jump in and decide what you think about every situation. You don't need to have an opinion at all. In the same way, not everything demands that you step in and offer advice, find a solution, or make efforts to fix what's in front of you (here, we see elements of *wu wei*—i.e., be 100 percent certain that something is truly broken before you decide that you're the one to fix it!).

Sometimes we make the worst errors in judgment because we were too quick to grab at an easy explanation or justification and didn't wait for the situation to unfold and mature at its own pace.

When you are clutching eagerly to "I have all the answers," that means you are no longer learning, no longer listening, and no longer alive to the truth of the situation. You no longer have a beginner's mind. Nina uses this tip when she calls a timeout on her important decision and just gives herself some space to think and contemplate, without the rush and compulsion to have quick, perfect answers for everything.

Lesson 2: Let go of the need to be right.

Nina's friends, family, and husband all have very strong ideas about the "right" thing for Nina to do. Without necessarily meaning to, they have imbued their opinions and preferences with strong moral assumptions, and Nina can't help but absorb some of these messages.

But what if she can just take a big step back and look at the situation for what it is, without the lens of "right" and "wrong"? She realizes that when she stops thinking of this choice as a pronouncement on her character, as a competition between her and others who have made different decisions, or even as something she has to explain or justify to people, then she notices she feels far more clarity about the situation. According to Ben Casnocha, "Others don't need to lose for me to win." What's more, there is no prize at the end of life for choosing the best, most objectively correct path.

One major insight Nina has is that even if the people in her world don't necessarily understand or approve of a choice she makes, it doesn't mean that she's wrong, or that they're wrong. In fact, once she removes their assumptions and hers from the equation, the whole thing starts to look a lot simpler.

Lesson 3: Assume you're an idiot.

One way to make a decision is to try to be as wise, rational, careful, and intelligent as you can be. Another way is to realize that no human can ever be all these things!

Take it as a given that you are limited in your thinking, a little self-serving, and that you have just as many poor ideas and stubborn little blind spots as anyone else. Take it as a given that you are missing some crucial information, and that the things that seem obvious and certain today may well not seem that way in five, ten, or fifteen years' time.

Rather than this being an exercise in self-humiliation, it's really about the relief that comes with not expecting yourself to have everything figured out. Instead of strenuously going over old evidence that already supports the viewpoint you've come to, stay open and curious enough to consider evidence that doesn't support your conclusion. Assume that it's possible to learn from other people—even and especially those you don't agree with or understand. Start from the assumption that you are missing something, and then become curious about what it might be.

Nina realizes that she may not have enough information about the decision she's facing. Rather than make assumptions about what she guesses is the case, she decides to gather cold hard evidence from a wide range of perspectives. She reaches out to a few people who have actually launched businesses in her industry, and she talks to them honestly about their experiences. She also talks to people who used to work in the industry but don't any longer. She chats with people who would be her ideal customer, but more importantly, she interviews those who definitely *wouldn't* buy her service, and tries to understand why.

Nina's process of adopting a beginner's mind brings her much clarity and focus. She is able to tune out the opinions and interference of others (as well-meaning as it is) and look at the choices ahead of her with a calm, detached, and curious mindset. The irony is that the more open-minded Nina is, and the longer she stays in the "I don't know" state of mind, the more valuable information she is gathering, and the more she learns.

This is the paradox of a beginner's mind: **It is the expert who ends up knowing so little,**

and the self-confessed beginner who ends up with true wisdom and learning.

- Adopt intellectual humility. You may have plenty of expertise, education, and accolades behind you, but forget about all of that and focus instead on what you *don't* know or understand.
- Confidence is overrated! Instead, be strong enough to ask for help, seek clarification, or pause long enough to understand the facts a little more clearly before making any pronouncements.
- Argue against yourself. You may be surprised at just how much you are assuming is correct simply because it's *you* who is doing the assuming.
- Ask yourself what choice you'd make if nobody else's opinions mattered. Also, ask what you would do if you didn't have to explain or justify yourself, or fulfill any expectations—yours or other people's.
- Finally, try to describe your situation or choice as a child would, or even as an alien from another planet might describe it. When all assumption and interpretation and bias is removed, what do you actually *see*?

Like so many of the mental models explored in this book, *shoshin* is not a method or a set of techniques, but rather an attitude. It means we embark on decision-making knowing that we do not have perfect knowledge or full understanding, and so we should adopt a position of open-minded humility. It's making respectful room for the unknown and softening the edges of our own ego and vanity so that we see things as they are . . . or as close to it as possible!

Summary

- For long-term decisions, consider Nietzsche's idea of eternal recurrence: that whatever you choose for yourself, try to imagine what it would be like to make that decision over and over again, eternally. Imagining that we may have to endure a consequence forever puts a different perspective on our long-term choices and pushes us to adopt radical acceptance, or *amor fati*, a love of one's fate.
- If you're facing a major life decision, but moral or practical approaches are not helping you gain any clarity, consider your desire and goal beyond good and bad. Create your own meaning and value rather than merely assuming the one given to you is adequate. Think about long-term consequences and the paths that unfold.

- Finally, acceptance is important: What if there is no heaven and hell waiting for us, but only this moment right now? Could we accept it all just as it is?
- Pascal's wager can be summarized: If God does exist and you believe in him, then you'll be rewarded in the afterlife. However, if you don't believe in God, and he does exist, then you will likely end up in eternal damnation. Therefore, it's worth believing just in case. We can use his insights on asymmetric payoffs, risk, and probability to help with more mundane decisions.
- Adopting a beginner's mindset means being willing to look at things as though for the first time, without the bias of expertise, assumption, or ego. Embracing what you don't know paradoxically makes you more effective at solving problems.

Chapter 4: Problem-Solving in Decision-Making

In this chapter, we are going to play around with ideological lenses that turn things upside down, back to front, or inside out. First, by considering *via negativa*—or the negative path—we will learn to remove elements from a problem or situation rather than attempting to add elements. And in our contemplation of the idea that "the map is not the territory," we will concern ourselves not with the virtues of our mental model, but with all the things that model *can't* do.

Finally, we'll look at the tale of Buridan's ass and turn the entire idea of problem-solving upside down: Sometimes, it's not a question of Choice A versus Choice B, but rather a comparison between choosing any choice versus remaining in a state of impotent indecision. Let's take a closer look.

***Via Negativa*—Subtraction as a Path to Truth**

"It is remarkable how much long-term advantage people like us have gotten by trying to be consistently not stupid, instead of trying to be very intelligent."

Charlie Munger

When we're faced with a tricky decision, we usually focus on one question: What should I do? Similarly, when solving a problem, we look at the situation and try to think of what we need to introduce to correct things. For example, we can't focus on our work, so we dream up ways to add more discipline or productivity; we lack purpose, so we try to find one; we see that we are ill and start to wonder about which medicine we can take or treatment we can receive.

All of these approaches, however, are **additive**. They're about putting in what we believe is lacking. This approach makes sense—in a confusing situation, we naturally know more about what's going wrong than what's going right, so that's where we focus our attention. But there is another, opposite approach we could take—we could think about what needs to be removed. This is a **subtractive** process and the essence of a mental model called *via negativa*, or "the negative way."

Much like Pascal's wager was initially offered as proof for the existence of God, the subtractive epistemology of *via negativa* was originally a theological exercise pondering the nature of God. The idea was that because God's infinite and supreme attributes could never be fully expressed by man, we could instead make more progress by expressing all the things that God is *not*.

By gradually eliminating from God's definition all the things that he is not, we approach the problem from the other direction. Not only is this easier for us mere mortals, but it helps us logically whittle away at possibilities until we are left with what must be true or accurate.

This approach is ancient, and a version is found in the Hindu Upanishads and Avadhuta Gita, where it is called *neti neti* (in Sanskrit नेति नेति), which translates to "not this, not that." To understand the nature of Brahman—i.e., the ultimate reality of the universe or God—we meditate on what Brahman isn't. **So, to better grasp the nature of something we don't**

know well and cannot calculate with any precision, we look at what we *do* know well and can calculate more clearly, and then work backward.

According to author Nassim Nicholas Taleb, *via negativa* is,

> "The principle that we know what is wrong with more clarity than what is right, and that knowledge grows by subtraction. Also, it is easier to know that something is wrong than to find the fix. Actions that remove are more robust than those that add because addition may have unseen, complicated feedback loops."

In a way, the entire scientific method proceeds via this negative route; in experiments, we do not seek to prove a hypothesis, only to disprove one. **We never arrive at truth so much as chip away at things we know for sure are false.** This is because one tiny negative observation can invalidate a positive statement. In Taleb's famous book *The Black Swan*, he explains how you can confidently say that all swans are white if you have seen millions of swans before, all white. Yet the observance of a single black swan is enough to completely invalidate the statement "all swans are white." In other words, disconfirmation is more powerful a tool than confirmation. The underlying philosophy of science is not proof, but falsification—i.e., the ability to say, "not this, not that."

Thus, there is a counter current flowing in the stream of popular advice and self-help out there: You can get further in life by simply committing yourself to identifying and avoiding mistakes (subtraction), than actively pursuing the positive (addition). In Elon Musk's words, your goal is not to seek truth directly, but "be less wrong."

Firing a poor team member in your company could have greater effects than finding ways to be more productive; avoiding smoking and drinking could have greater effects than worrying about the best workout program or nutritional supplement; knowing how to retain the friends you have could have greater effects than figuring out how to be charming and likeable enough to win new friends.

Via negativa is an interesting mental model because it asks us to look at things in precisely the opposite way we might intuitively guess we should. Michelangelo, when asked about his method for creating his famous statue of David, said, "It's simple. I just remove everything that is not David." The Hippocratic Oath, too, rests on the spirit of *via negativa*, saying that a doctor's first job is in what he doesn't do: "first, do no harm," or, as it appears in earlier versions, "I will abstain from all intentional wrongdoing and harm." In other words, the first job of a good doctor is to "be less wrong."

In earlier chapters we explored the value of "sitting with" a problem rather than rushing in as quickly as possible to "fix" it before you even understand it in the first place. Arguably, much of the power of *wu wei* and flowing with the harmony of nature may come down to this: being curious about the failure itself (all the empty space that isn't David), rather than the success you might quickly heap on top of it (the glorious final form of David).

With the mental model of elimination and subtraction, we not only identify what is or could be, but we also train ourselves to focus. Steve Jobs said,

> "People think focus means saying yes to the thing you've got to focus on. But that's not what it means at all. It means saying no to the hundred other good ideas that there are. You have to pick carefully. I'm actually as proud of the things we haven't done as the things I have done. Innovation is saying no to 1,000 things."

In the same way, **_via negativa_ can help us identify boundaries and limits, as well as zoom in on our most important values and goals**. Instead of asking, "What do I want?" you can go about it the other way and identify all those things you know for certain you don't want. Then look at the shape of the thing that is left over after you've eliminated all of that! Logically, *this* must be what you want.

As with Pascal's wager, whether or not this approach is useful for discovering the nature of God or not is beside the point—what matters is that it's still a useful tool for helping us discover the nature of all sorts of other situations.

The early theologians might have pondered God's attributes, thinking that God cannot be limited, he cannot be evil, he cannot be a man, he cannot be confused, he cannot be unintelligent, and so on. To take things even further, as was often the case in using the *neti neti* meditation, we could start to unravel duality itself and arrive at the profoundly ineffable, non-dual nature of God or underlying reality. Much like Descartes discovered, when you continue to hack away, what you are ultimately left with is simply the perceiving consciousness beneath it all—i.e., I meditate, therefore I am!

Hacking Away at the Inessential

Let's see how we can put the mental model of *via negativa* to practical use. Though simple, the mental switch from positive to negative is often subtle and difficult to do when you're in the heat of the moment—i.e., you're facing a complicated decision or can't see your way out of a problem. Consider the following examples.

- When writing an essay or article, instead of asking what you can add, or how you can bring in more color, persuasion, or articulation, simply ask what is already there but needs to be removed. Hunt out errors, trim away redundancies, and delete any unnecessary repetition. Your essay will be better without you adding anything.
- When faced with a challenging decision, first check to see if any of the potential options should simply be eliminated. Get rid of noise and distractions.
- When trying to make improvements to your lifestyle, don't worry too much about spending money, time, or effort on adding something new until you've gone over your existing lifestyle and identified things that can be removed. For example, rather than buying special equipment and ingredients to make healthy smoothies and juices, just commit to not drinking as much alcohol, soda, and coffee as you currently do.

- When trying to make improvements in your business, rather than focusing exclusively on profits, also spend some time thinking about unnecessary expenses or waste.

For a more complicated example, imagine that you are trying to figure out a career path and are repeatedly finding yourself stumped. What do you want to do with your life? You're not sure. You have a few skills and talents, a few opportunities it seems smart to capitalize on, a few possibilities, a few limitations . . . but nothing is really striking you as the right way forward.

This would be a perfect time to switch your lens and consider a *via negativa* approach: Instead of trying to *find* your values, what about simply removing everything you absolutely know isn't valuable to you, and which doesn't work for you?

So, let's say you sit down with a piece of paper and brainstorm in an open-ended way first. You think about all the jobs you've had in the past, good and bad. What made the good ones so enjoyable, and what made the bad ones so unpleasant? You note down a few things, then move on to another interesting question: What is the absolute worst possible job you can imagine yourself having? Most importantly, *why* would this be so bad?

You really get into the flow of things (isn't it always so much easier to know what you don't like than it is to know what you do like?). You look at this long list of tasks, environments, kinds of people, skill sets, and so on that don't appeal for one reason or another.

Now, the obvious part—looking at what you've written, what you can infer from all these things you don't value? What are their natural opposites? If you despise being micromanaged, for example, that might suggest that you enjoy working independently and taking initiative. If you have in the past felt most stressed at the prospect of having to rush, this might tell you that you value having the time to produce quality work, or that you have a strong perfectionist streak and like to take pride in your work. If you hate working indoors, this suggests you might like working outdoors, and so on.

In the end, you may not have a perfect job description of the ideal role for you, but you will have a list of its attributes. You can then use this to cross reference against the options in front of you, and it may help you focus (recall the *ikigai* Venn diagram). It may not be a commonly held opinion, but sometimes it *is* enough to simply set the goal of avoiding something unpleasant, rather than explicitly aiming for something pleasant.

Finally, this approach can help mitigate overly perfectionistic tendencies—i.e., it's usually not rational to delay making a decision until the *perfect* option comes along. Rather, we get further if we eliminate the clearly unsuitable options and then get to work with what's left over.

Remember that the Map Is Not the Territory

"The map is not the territory, the word is not the thing it describes. Whenever the map is confused with the territory, a 'semantic disturbance' is set up in the organism. The disturbance continues until the limitation of the map is recognized."

— *Alfred Korzybski*

Sebastian has a difficult decision to make. His girlfriend has given him an ultimatum: Either they commit to one another and settle down, or they break up so she can seek out someone who eventually wants to get married and have children. On the one hand, Sebastian considers himself a free spirit and absolutely loathes the idea of being tied down or limited in any way. But on the other hand, he recognizes that his girlfriend has a point: They're both at the stage in their lives where it's natural to start thinking of the longer term.

What should Sebastian do? In his mind, the decision goes like this: freedom versus love. He can only have one or the other. But he values both! He's in a real pickle. He wants to be his own free person, individualized and at liberty to always choose his own way, but he *also* wants the comforts of being in a relationship, and all the benefits that brings.

He seeks out the advice of his close friend. He essentially asks this friend, "What should I choose here—companionship or independence?" But the friend responds in a way that completely shows up Sebastian's "semantic disturbance." He answers: "Maybe you should stop thinking of those things as mutually exclusive opposites."

Sebastian has framed his decision/problem in a certain way and is fretting about his possible choices from *within* that frame; his friend points out to him that the problem may really lie with the frame itself. Mathematician Alfred Korzybski would understand this, as it was he who coined the phrase "The map is not the territory." In other words, the mental model that Sebastian is using to understand his life is *not the same thing* as his life. Once he realizes this, he can start to make headway in this dilemma.

Korzybski's idea is an extended metaphor. According to him, **there is the territory (reality) and there are our maps (our models, interpretations, understandings, and explanations) about that reality.** We need maps to chart a way through the wilderness, but we encounter problems when we forget that our maps are manmade and can be wrong. If we are using a map and discover one day that there is a mountain in the world where the map told us there was a valley, then the problem is not the mountain in front of us, but our faulty map.

Korzybski made a few more important points. Not only can a map be wrong without you realizing it, but good maps can become outdated over time. Maps are a tool, but an imperfect one; they are *necessarily limited* and a simplification of the territory they represent. In other words, the map can never really fully grasp the rich, three-dimensional nature of the territory.

We can use Korzybski's idea for more abstract representations of reality (such as in science or mathematics), but we can also use it in our own lives, where the "maps" we use include our attitudes, explanations, beliefs, expectations, assumptions, and biases. **When we encounter a kind of dissonance between our picture of the world and the world itself, we encounter a learning opportunity**—or a crisis, if we are unaware of what is happening.

When we have a mismatch between the map and reality, we must make a choice. Returning to Sebastian's case, how might his problem be solved? He could decide that his girlfriend is forcing him to behave in a way that doesn't work for him, and so he breaks up with her. This is akin to choosing to keep the map—i.e., the mental model that frames love in opposition to freedom. Sometimes, when people's "cognitive maps" are threatened, they respond by avoidance (just don't acknowledge the mismatch) or by confirmation bias (try to interpret dissonant stimuli in a way that fits the map). Sebastian could angrily say that his girlfriend is trying to trap him, frame her ultimatum as controlling, and call the breakup a narrow escape from a miserable, compromised existence.

The other choice Sebastian could make is to update his map—i.e., take his friend's advice and become curious about what it might look like to consider an option where he could be free to be himself while *also* being in a committed relationship. This is akin to throwing out one map and creating another—hopefully one that better represents the nature of the territory in question. **This is a way of solving the problem by stepping outside of it.** Sebastian realizes that his attitude to relationships is distorted and comes from internalized messages he received growing up. It's a little like realizing that a certain map might have been useful back when you were a teenager, but now is outdated because it doesn't show all the new roads that have since been built.

Our perception is never identical to reality. Ever. But we can always create closer and closer approximations if we are willing to become curious about those uncomfortable moments where our estimations about the world don't quite add up anymore. We have to be willing to learn. Very often, life's biggest problems are solved at this level—i.e., the level of our mental representations of a problem and not with the minor details of the problem itself.

Whenever you make an abstraction of something, you introduce the possibility of error. This is not a problem as long as we are aware that this is what is happening and prepared to update when necessary. Again, we see the value of a "beginner's mind." It is the expert who is most likely to use old maps that once worked but now don't. In a sense, this entire book is about building a supply of different maps. Just as there are different types of literal maps—political, topographical, nautical—you can also get completely different perspectives on the same phenomena, each highlighting a different aspect. The value of having this map inventory is not in being able to compare them and find the best ones, but to constantly remain aware of the fact of them being maps in the first place. The *real phenomenon* out there is, in many ways, ungraspable, indescribable.

Sometimes we may fall into the trap of seeking out territory that fits the map we already have. If we allow avoidance and confirmation bias to guide us, and consistently double down with our chosen maps when faced with any dissonance, then we may find ourselves ultimately creating more confusion and unhappiness in the long run. For Sebastian, this may mean breaking up with his girlfriend and unconsciously seeking out a woman who he believes will not try to trap him in the same way.

This means his map deliberately leads him to women who are just as unwilling to commit (perhaps they are using a similar map to his own). But this leads to a seemingly never-ending string of chaotic and superficial relationships that never leave Sebastian feeling cared for and secure. His girlfriends, being noncommittal, tend to cheat or lose interest over time. "See? You really *do* have to choose between love or freedom!" It's as if his map has become a self-fulfilling prophecy. Models can, after all, create their own reality over time.

In the world of Sebastian's map, a particular story always plays out the same way. No matter where he turns or who he dates, the picture always looks the same. It's only when he grows tired of the limitations of his map/worldview that he can start to imagine something else. And when he changes his map, he can suddenly "see" so much of what he wasn't aware of before. Like switching from a simple street map to a colorful topographic map showing contours and forests, it's as though the world he inhabits itself changes.

One day, with a new map, Sebastian may be able to challenge his assumption that intimacy in relationships means loss of freedom and loss of self. But this magical "promised land," this place where love doesn't cost your individuality, is something he can only find if he uses the right map to navigate a way there.

More practically speaking, we can use the map analogy to keep our decision-making clear and as error-free as possible. Here are a few ideas:

Make No Assumptions

The biggest mistake you can make is to assume that you can't possibly make a mistake. Frequently check the usefulness and accuracy of the maps you're using. When something seems a little off or inexplicable, pause and try to understand if the problem is the way you're thinking about things. One great way to uncover the (often unconscious) maps you may be using is to look for words like "should" or "must" in your thinking. Double check if these assumptions, demands, or expectations are actually founded. **Look for evidence.** Is there any proof or are you just using a set of assumptions and guesses because it's what you've always used, and it worked once before?

Ask Who Made the Map

Let's be honest: A lot of us are using old, outdated maps we inherited from other people. Sebastian, for example, picked up his map from his father, who always made disparaging comments about marriage and modeled a particular approach to dating that Sebastian couldn't help but assume as his own.

If you're using someone else's map, consider what their motivation was. Is it *your* motivation? Might you be better served by something that reflects your focus, goals, and values? On the other hand, maybe the person who made the map is you—only a younger version of you. **Just because something worked in the past, however, doesn't mean it will still work now.**

Triangulate Your Worldview

The more maps you have, the better. None of them in isolation tell you everything there is to know, but together they can start to paint a more vivid picture. Sebastian can do this by asking the advice and opinions of plenty of different kinds of people—not just the kind of people who are likely to be using the exact same map he is.

Can he speak to men who have the opposite view of freedom and relationships? Even better, can he set aside his own interpretations for a moment and take a closer look at the map that his own girlfriend is using? Looking at the way she is making meaning may help him see hidden contours and outlines in his own map that he hadn't thought of before.

Get Your Ego Out of the Equation

It's tempting to construct a map and then strongly identify with it. We can become quite attached to our abstract models of the world, defending them ferociously as if we ourselves were being attacked. Vanity might mean we cling a little too tightly to a representation of the world that we personally find more flattering, comforting, or palatable—despite what the evidence actually says. On the other hand, we may become fond of our mental models simply because they're ours, and we don't like to imagine that we've got it somewhat wrong.

Korzybski was making a point about mathematics and the more fundamental perils of abstract representation, but in everyday life, we are more at risk of emotional dishonesty than we are intellectual dishonesty. That is, we use certain maps not because they are objectively the most useful or rational, but because they satisfy some emotional need. We may construct for ourselves, like Sebastian did, a map of the world that is distorted by fear (or laziness or anger or pride). **Getting our ego out of the equation means we allow ourselves to let go of what isn't working and be more curious about what might work better.**

When the Map and the Territory Differ, Follow the Territory

Experiencing a "semantic disturbance" (i.e., discomfort from realizing that your theory and reality don't line up well) is not a problem—it's data. As Nassim Taleb says, "A model might show you some risks, but not the risks of using it. Moreover, models are built on a finite set of parameters, while reality affords us infinite sources of risks."

When something isn't working, get curious about the potential risks of using your model that are now being revealed to you. See the mismatch as an opportunity to adjust the map to fit, rather than double down and reinterpret the territory so it justifies the map. For example, let's say you're struggling with "imposter syndrome." Your map tells you that there are high risks to putting yourself out there, but it doesn't help you calculate the risks of using this map in the first place (opportunity cost, underachieving, low self-esteem, etc.).

A certain worldview may have habituated you to thinking about risk and reward in a certain way, but that worldview itself may expose you to certain risks. When in doubt, assume you're wrong, look for evidence, and get curious about your mental tools.

Buridan's Ass

"Commitment is an act, not a word."
Jean-Paul Sartre

The story goes like this: One day a hungry and thirsty donkey is walking down the road. It sees a cool trough of water on the left side, and on the right side, it sees a tasty-looking hay pile. It turns to walk toward the water but then has a change of heart. Maybe it wants the hay first. It turns toward the hay, but then it can't quite decide. Is it thirstier or hungrier? Which option is more attractive, really?

After endless dawdling and time wasting, the donkey dies in the middle of the road, satisfying neither his hunger nor his thirst. He dies, the story tells us, not because of a lack of good options, but because of indecision.

This story has a long history—it was potentially popular even in Aristotle's day—but the above version is named Buridan's ass after the French philosopher Jean Buridan. The tale is meant to point to a particular kind of human foible—indecision. If the donkey realized it could enjoy one choice and then the other, it could have had both. However, its behavior is evidence of a kind of all-or-nothing thinking. It's the failure to recognize that a "bad choice" is not the end of the world—life goes on afterward, and you can always choose differently in the future.

Besides this, Buridan's ass could also be accused of a kind of short-sighted perfectionism: In wanting to make a final, optimal choice there and then, he ultimately delays making *any* choice, which is actually far worse than making an error, learning from it, and simply moving on.

No discussion about optimal decision-making would be complete without thinking about the nature of choice itself,

and the cost of indecision. If you've ever felt stuck between two (or more!) choices, you will have felt this dilemma acutely. On the one hand, having choices feels like a good thing—our culture values autonomy, free will, and self-direction. But not only does this raise the stakes on the decision we do eventually make, it poses a question: How much choice is too much? How long till we start resembling Buridan's ass, who is not empowered by choice but crippled by it?

The world today is richer in information than it ever has been, and choice (or perhaps the illusion of choice) is everywhere. The paradox is that people are not happier or any more confident in their choices. Many of us feel immobilized and overwhelmed.

Psychologist and choice expert Barry Schwartz explains the results of his "jam study":

> "When researchers set up [in a gourmet food store] a display featuring a line of exotic, high-quality jams, customers who came by could taste samples, and they were given a coupon for a dollar off if they bought a jar. In one condition of the study, 6 varieties of the jam were available for tasting. In another, 24

varieties were available. In either case, the entire set of 24 varieties was available for purchase. The large array of jams attracted more people to the table than the small array, though in both cases people tasted about the same number of jams on average. When it came to buying, however, a huge difference became evident. Thirty percent of the people exposed to the small array of jams actually bought a jar; only 3 percent of those exposed to the large array of jams did so."

What Schwartz's study tells us is that **an overabundance of choice can actually lead to "choice paralysis" or a reduction in decisive action.** This is certainly something to consider if we wish to become better decision-makers. Choosing is stressful. It takes time, energy, and cognitive resources.

What's more, having more options doesn't mean we necessarily have more information about the optimal course of action. There are still unknowns, and usually no way of weighing them up or comparing them so that you could confidently say, "This is it. This right here is the *best* choice for me." Never being able to arrive at that conclusion keeps you drifting in a stressful state of indecision.

Social media floods our attention with images of alternative careers, paths, and lifestyles. Self-help books suggest that there is always a happier, richer life out there, beckoning us if only we'd choose it. Influencers, politicians, talking heads, and assorted demagogues paint rich pictures of other ways to be, to think, to live. They continually present to us the same implicit question: What do you choose? Which one do you want?

Just like Buridan's ass dying in the middle of the road without ever having actually made a choice, we may be paralyzed ourselves by this deluge of choice, overwhelmed and desperately trying to optimize, all whilst never making a single choice either way.

The solution to the ass's problem is simple: Just make a choice. Any choice. Maybe it matters what you choose, *but maybe it doesn't*. Maybe life doesn't rest on this single choice, but rather a long string of choices made after one another—a string that will only ever begin with you acting.

Choice impacts the kinds of jam we taste and buy, but it also impacts the bigger arcs of our lives—the work we do, our relationships, the places we live, and what we do there. What Buridan's ass teaches us is that **the only truly "wrong decision" is indecision**.

Consider an example, who we'll call Jean in honor of Jean Buridan. Jean is launching a new coaching business but spending a lot of time doing "research" on exactly the niche she'd like to focus on. She's done a few courses, read a few books, and chatted with a few experts. She still can't decide, however, whether she wants to focus on being a fitness coach for new mothers who want to lose the baby weight, or to work with older women who want to be fitter in their retirement years.

She puts off launching her coaching business until she's figured it out. She also finds herself dawdling on other smaller choices: How much should she charge? What should she call herself? Where should she advertise her services? What should the font on her business cards be?

As you can imagine, Jean is getting close to "dying in the middle of the road" in terms of her business. In fact, she dawdles for an entire year. She eventually does make a choice and, lo and behold, it's not the ideal choice anyway. In other words, even after mulling over it for ages, she still doesn't make the "perfect choice." She settles on a niche, a fee, a name, a business card font . . . and yet all of these choices get reworked over time anyway.

This is important: *Dawdling and indecision do not enhance decision quality. All they do is waste precious time.*

Let's take a look at Jean's path:

1. Plan, "research," and dawdle *for a whole year*
2. Take action
3. See results of action and adjust accordingly

Time spent: a year. **Effort level:** high. **Learning opportunities:** just one.

Let's take a look at another potential path:

1. Do a cursory scan of possibilities for a week or so
2. Take action
3. See the results of action and adjust accordingly
4. Repeat steps 2 and 3

Time spent: a few weeks. **Effort level:** moderate. **Learning opportunities:** several.

Thinking in terms of mental models, we can see the hidden cost of the mental model that says, "Delay action until you're 100 percent sure of an ideal outcome." The cost, of course, is time but also lost opportunities to learn—after all, sometimes the only way we can know whether a choice is the right choice is to try it and see what happens.

While we could spend an eternity in limbo trying to answer the question "Which font will people like best?" it's easier and more rational to simply make a decision—any decision—and observe the result. The cost of *not* acting in this case is far, far higher than the cost of acting, gathering data, adjusting, and then acting again.

Time is valuable. And most decisions are not as final as they may seem (unless, of course, they are Type 1 decisions we mentioned earlier. Truly irreversible decisions are not as common as we think, however). Jean may fritter away time and energy trying to optimize, and all the while she is not actually acquiring any more information that would make the choice any easier. Her "research" is not really research at all, but avoidance, delay, and procrastination.

The Power of Commitment

Here's a truth that we seldom like to acknowledge: **We never have all the information needed to make the perfect decision**. We cannot predict the future, and sometimes chance and randomness take over. We can make educated guesses, we can work with probabilities and likelihoods, but at some point, we have to make a kind of leap of faith and act despite not really knowing if it's the right move (more on that later). The trap of "analysis paralysis" is that it keeps us stuck in optimizing mode. This is a fundamentally impotent place to be.

On the other hand, taking action keeps things moving. We open ourselves up to new experiences, and we start to gather data. We receive feedback. We test our assumptions and see how they fare in the "real world." The world responds to our efforts, and we have the chance to adjust. We start to realize that the success of our life doesn't rest on just one or two major decisions, but a whole network of millions of tiny iterative decisions, one built on the other.

If the donkey had chosen one or the other option, then he might have realized that upon choosing, a whole new world suddenly opens up. He can now see that another choice is possible. A sequence of choices becomes available to him: first one thing, then the other. **In other words, his choice itself changed the field of available options.** His choice, even if it was the "wrong" one, was still a way to act on his environment and have an effect on it. And this change allowed him to make the next decision.

The surprise is that mistakes and "wrong choices" actually have value, too. They yield data and offer opportunities to learn. They shift the landscape of choices. They may even shift the way you are looking at that same landscape. Things *move*. However, if you stay stuck in indecision, that landscape slowly grows stale. No new data enters the picture. You end up chewing over the same bits of information again and again—and that starts to look like rumination and worry rather than problem-solving.

If the story of Buridan's ass is resonating for you, it may be that you need to shift your focus from "optimal action" toward the value of action itself . . . *any action*. Sometimes, we find that **motivation and clarity only appear for us *after* we've already chosen a path and committed to it**. Our sense of certainty and dedication to a choice actually comes as a side effect of us having made the choice. There is a freedom, paradoxically, in narrowing your options. There is a relief in knowing that, essentially, you don't have the choice anymore: Your path, then, is not to identify the optimal choice, but to find a way to *optimize that choice*. Big difference.

Commit to a path. This doesn't mean that you are doomed to carry out the consequences of a decision for the rest of your life. Rather, *see commitment as a willingness to engage.* To continually take action, ask questions, and learn from your experiences. To commit to staying open-minded and having a scientific approach—that is, to using action to gather data, test assumptions, and arrive at a good outcome actively and purposefully.

This view of commitment sees action not as something we do once we have perfect knowledge and certainty, but rather the *way* we find that certainty and knowledge over time, through trial and error. Our opening Jean-Paul Sartre quote tells us that **"Commitment is an act."** Conversely, acting is commitment. But this committing action does not reduce our freedom and cut short our horizon of possibilities, but rather opens them up. Buridan's ass is least free when he has the most options, but most free when he breaks out of indecision and takes action. To be less like Buridan's ass, try to remember:

- You seldom benefit from more options and choices. Keep things simple.
- Do one thing, then the other. Don't multitask, and don't get into the state of mind where you see the success of your entire life as resting on a single choice. Think of goals and tasks serially, rather

than in parallel. The donkey can only eat/drink one thing at a time.
- If it's not an irreversible Type 1 decision, any action is usually better than no action at all.
- Settle for a good-enough outcome and let go of the expectation that things turn out perfectly.

Summary

- A mental model called *via negativa*, or "the negative way," emphasizes what we can remove from a situation rather than add. To better grasp the nature of something we don't know well and cannot calculate with any precision, we look at what we *do* know well and can calculate more clearly, and then work backward.
- We never arrive at truth so much as chip away at things we know for sure are false; a variation on the principle is to "be less wrong" and avoid errors before striving for accomplishments. *Via negativa* can help us identify boundaries and limits, as well as focus on our values and goals.
- Remember that the territory (reality) is not the same as our map (our models, interpretations, understandings, and explanations) of that reality. When map and territory don't align, consider it a

learning opportunity and adjust the map. Maps are necessarily simplified and limited, they can be wrong, and they can be outdated. Make no assumptions, ask about who made the map and why, and consistently "triangulate" your beliefs against alternatives.
- An overabundance of choice can actually lead to "choice paralysis" and costly indecision. The story of Buridan's ass teaches us that sometimes action, *any* action, is preferable to stalling indefinitely. Dawdling does not enhance decision quality; what it does is waste precious time.
- We never have all the information needed to make the perfect decision. Rather than trying to endlessly gather data, instead commit, take action, learn from your actions, and adjust as you go. Mistakes and wrong choices have value, too, and are valid ways to act on the environment and change things.

Chapter 5: Embracing the Unknown in Decision-Making

In our final chapter, we face directly a part of decision-making that we have so far only hinted at: uncertainty and the unknown. Decision-making would be far, far easier if we always knew the outcome of every choice and could accurately predict every consequence. But of course, we can't. While being able to weigh up costs and payoffs is a useful skill, it's really the presence of the unknown, of that unmeasurable X factor, that most stumps the best of us.

How do we get around the fact that there are simply things that we cannot grasp or understand? How can we act wisely without complete knowledge? In this final chapter, we will use our microscope more like a telescope and take the broadest possible view of human free will and choice. We will consider whether there is any potential for freedom and meaning in a world that we can only ever partially understand.

Transformational Change and the "Vampire" Analogy

Buridan's ass only had to decide whether to go for the water or the hay first. Human beings in real life have far, far more complex decisions to make! The decisions most likely to stump us are the big, life-altering ones: whether to marry or divorce, whether to take the leap and move to some far-flung country to start over, whether to commit to an occupation that will require years of dedication and learning, whether to have children, how many children to have...

With these kinds of decisions, it can feel almost impossible to know what we're really dealing with. In fact, Laurie Ann Paul, professor of philosophy at the University of North Carolina at Chapel Hill, says that this feature of big decisions is something we should really lean into. To illustrate the real nature of what she calls "transformative decisions," she points to the story of how a vampire becomes a vampire.

Let's say someone comes to you one day and offers you the choice to become a vampire—they will bite your neck, and in that moment, you will be set on the irreversible path of being a vampire for all eternity. There's no going back. Let's say there are some attractive benefits to being a vampire, but also some drawbacks. It's a decision worth considering carefully.

Now, you could read plenty of books on what to expect after being turned into a vampire, you could chat with vampires and ask them their opinions, you could look at vampire statistics and read firsthand accounts of those who both regretted their decision and those who were glad they chose what they did ... but Laurie Ann Paul says that none of this really matters.

Why? Because once you are turned into a vampire, you are no longer yourself. You are a vampire. And from that moment, everything will look different to you. **You have undergone a *transformational change*—and by definition this is not something you can predict your response to.**

You cannot know what you will make of a decision until you make it—and by that time it may be too late. In the same way, getting married/divorced, having a child, moving to another country, and so on are all precisely the kinds of decisions that will fundamentally change your frame of reference. Your values, your understanding, your experience, your perception, and the way you make meaning will be changed by the decision itself.

So, as a human offered vampirehood, the prospect of immortality might have seemed pretty cool, but when you actually *are* immortal, you are suddenly privy to a range of perceptions and experiences that were not accessible to you when you were a human. Add time to the mix and you can see how these fundamental changes may keep compounding . . . while being a vampire might have had its appeal to you as a 25-year-old, that may change when you are a 125-year-old vampire, and indeed change again when you are 525!

The point here is that **experience always changes us**. We are making an error if we assume that the future version of ourselves post-decision will be the same as the version we are living right now. Sometimes, we have to actually experience the consequences of an action firsthand to really understand the value of that action. Before that, we are only making guesses and conjectures.

So instead of asking ourselves, "Which of these choices does my current self like best?" we could ask, "What kind of future self do I want to be? In what ways do I want to change in the future?" This way, we are acknowledging that change will in fact happen, and that the way we perceive and rate that change may also be different from the way we are doing it now.

Paul offers another example. Imagine you have never eaten durian fruit. This is an exotic and polarizing delicacy that some people describe as absolutely disgusting, and others as the most delicious fruit in the world. One day you get the chance to sample durian fruit. You have the option to eat a regular fruit you already know you like (let's say pineapple) or the chance to try durian.

The problem is you are facing what Paul calls an "epistemological inaccessibility"—there's just a black hole where any information about the taste of durian would be. You can get plenty of other people's opinions, but you will never know what it's like to experience the taste yourself... until you taste it. There is no way for you to measure the value of eating durian. It's a total unknown, so it short-circuits any method you could use to calculate risk and benefit.

Now, this might look pretty pessimistic. How on earth can we make decisions under these conditions? How can we adopt a "trial and error" approach in the face of irreversible and high-stakes decisions?

While Paul is coming at the question from a rather academic and philosophical perspective, we can keep our considerations more pragmatic. The fact that human beings change along with the decisions they make only becomes a problem if we're unwilling to acknowledge the fact and factor it into our decision-making process. Here are a few things to keep in mind if you're facing what might be a transformational decision:

Acknowledge the Irreversibility of the Decision

This is not as scary as it may seem at first. Think of it this way: The irreversibility of a decision is itself likely to seem different to you from the other side—i.e., once you've already made that decision.

Many people find that making a big decision tends to bring an immediate sense of relief precisely *because* there is now no longer a question of going back. While pre-decision this may have caused anxiety, the fact is that post-decision you may feel very differently. In other words, irreversibility usually seems a bigger deal to people before they've made the decision.

Seek Guidance from Those Who Have Been There

Once you've acknowledged the fundamental inability to guess how you'll actually feel until after you've made the choice, you can start to manage this blind spot consciously. Asking other people about their experiences will never make the mystery any less of a mystery, but it can help you make a more informed, more relaxed, and more confident choice . . . and it can help you set up contingency plans for once you've made the decision.

If your big decision is whether to have children or not (or when to have them, or how many to have), then you might spend some time talking to people who are already parents, from those who found the decision easy to those who were filled with doubt but chose to go ahead anyway. What do they wish they had known before? What assumptions did they make that they now realize were unfounded?

Deliberately ask for their advice and try to absorb what they say through the perspective of your possible future self—not your present self. Even if all this advice-seeking yields no additional data about the decision at hand, it will make you feel more able to take the initiative. You will know that whatever happens post-decision, you really can rest assured that you did the best you could given the limits of your knowledge at the time. That will go a long way to reducing the risk of regret.

Speaking of regret, use other people's advice to help prepare a contingency plan. You cannot be sure if you'll find parenthood a breeze or an absolute nightmare, but in the case it turns out to be a nightmare, how can you prepare to offset the worst of it? By thinking this way, you are taking back some of your life from the hands of fate and empowering yourself to be a more proactive agent in how your life unfolds.

Realize that It's a Journey, Not a Single Moment

Some decisions in life come down to a single discrete choice in a single moment, no doubt about it. But most decisions, even the high-stakes ones, are not set up like this. Our life is made up of a series of evolving and iterative choices. Even if we do make a serious error, it's seldom the end of our ability to keep choosing, to change things, or to act differently in the future (despite what grumpy old Nietzsche might have said).

Take the pressure off yourself by realizing that no single decision is singlehandedly determining the outcome of your entire life. Consequences take time to unfold and can be negotiated. Few things are black and white, and even if you can't take a decision back, you actually have almost infinite ability to accept, manage, and grow into the consequences of your decisions. Relaxing into this process means knowing that choice-and-consequence is a dance that is constantly evolving (remember the cloak of karma you weave around yourself?). No matter how final a decision may feel, truly you will have plenty of opportunities to reconsider your values, your goals, and your perceptions.

Transformational change can seem pretty scary, but really, it's exactly what we want—we *want* to be able to take action that genuinely has the power to change our world completely; otherwise action wouldn't mean very much, right?

The profundity of our ability to choose and change our world brings us back to the idea of *amor fati*, and having the courage to embrace our existence, whatever its twists and turns. Even if you make a big decision filled with doubt, fear, and uncertainty, rest assured that in time, perhaps even very soon, the entire thing may look very, very different to you. Trust in that process.

Taking that Leap of Faith

"Life can only be understood backwards; but it must be lived forwards."

Soren Kierkegaard

As we near the end of our book and explore broader and more abstract mental models that we can use in our decision-making, we start to approach the furthest reaches of the faith-reason continuum. In this section we'll explore the mental model proposed by Danish philosopher Soren Kierkegaard, namely the idea of a "leap of faith."

In the previous section, we saw philosopher Laurie Ann Paul wrack her brain over the fundamental unknowable nature of the future. We saw her wrestle over how we can never truly stand back in complete rational detachment from the world in order to analyze our choices, because we are always *in* that world, and every choice we make has the chance of drastically changing us, as well as changing the way that we think about change.

Kierkegaard's approach is a little different. He endorses *a deliberate choice to embrace all those things beyond reason and empirical evidence.* Stepping into the unknown this way, he argues, is more fittingly a question of faith. Here, **faith is defined not**

as a kind of belief, but rather an act—that is, a decision to choose or accept something that lies beyond our ability to prove, explain, or understand through logic and reason. For Kierkegaard, this is not just a question of religious or spiritual matters (although that was primary to his thinking) but also a question of living wisely in a world where uncertainty is baked in.

There will always be limitations to reason and logic, Kierkegaard says. Rather than faith being some kind of reluctant concession, however, or a kind of temporary bin where we store everything we haven't quite figured out yet, we can see faith almost as a necessary and valuable approach to making sense of life.

This way of thinking challenges more traditional models of acquiring knowledge and acknowledges the value of subjective experience—can't we "know" and understand the world through our own personal commitments, our choice to adopt a worldview all our own, and our bravery in acting despite incomplete knowledge?

Faith is a strange thing to define. For Kierkegaard, it represented a quality a little like trust, devotion, or loyalty. His work influenced various postmodern and existentialist thinkers, who saw that the choice to believe was actually a powerful act of human freedom—something beautiful, even. Rather than faith being the kind of conviction that comes with a belief or a certainty in a fact, it is a choice and a decision—one made in the absence of conviction. What's more, it's not limited to religion, but applies any time where reason and evidence don't necessarily bring us any clarity.

This is why it is a "leap"—one lurches into the unknown and voluntarily takes the risk. The leap itself cannot be explained or justified by reason. It is an act that can only be experienced—"as you start to walk on the way, the way appears," according to Sufi poet Rumi. The result, Kierkegaard says, is a life lived with more commitment, passion, and purpose—albeit one where rationality, infallibility, and certainty are somewhat sacrificed. If you were to take a look at the decisions facing you in life right now, but you acknowledged deep down that there were **no guarantees** either way, how might it change your approach?

Leaping into the unknown can sometimes feel like a radical, even reckless act, but it really springs from the deep understanding that *we are all already in this position anyway*. We may have more or less convincing illusions to help us justify and rationalize our actions, but when it comes down to the truly "big questions," who of us can honestly say we have all the required information to act?

While grand transformational decisions can seem threatening, we can also reframe them as great moments of evolution, transcendence, and meaning. For some, the existential courage to have faith is one of humanity's most defining features.

Does this mean we should throw reason and logic out the window? Of course not.

Faith and reason may be mutually exclusive, but one can support the other. Pascal, for example, can set up logical arguments for why one ought to believe in God just in case, but this line of reasoning may follow alongside and precipitate a more intimate, intuitive, and personal negotiation of faith. **Beyond what might be true or false, reasonable or unreasonable, we can allow ourselves to explore those realms where we ask, "Regardless of everything, what do I *CHOOSE*?"**

This is the realm of values, personal ethics, individual perspectives, worldviews, intuition, ambiguity, even beauty. Can we not only embrace uncertainty, but find a way to live with it permanently?

Let's return to an example we encountered earlier in the book—the story of Sebastian, who was feeling (one could say almost existentially) threatened by the prospect of commitment to his girlfriend. One way of understanding Sebastian's dilemma is to see it in terms of fundamental uncertainty. "Is this the woman I should commit to for the rest of my life?" is simply a question none of us can answer. Sebastian could decide that despite the ample risks, despite not knowing how it will all work out, and despite his fear and hesitation, he *will* nevertheless choose to commit because this is the outcome he wants to make real for himself.

He takes a leap of faith into the unknown. He makes the radical choice to love his girlfriend anyway, completely, and to commit to her fully, even recklessly, despite everything. This is not a choice that can be rationalized or explained. There is no "reason" for it other than his desire to make it so.

This is not a choice he arrives at by compiling a cost-benefit chart or consulting divorce statistics. Rather, it may be a private commitment that Sebastian comes to within himself one day after a long night of contemplation. He is not saying "yes" to a life of certain happiness with his girlfriend. He is saying "yes" to life, his life, in whatever form it takes. He does not know how it will turn out. But he takes the leap anyway.

The irony, of course, is that having this kind of total commitment may be the one thing that best prepares Sebastian for a happy marriage. Because he can honestly say that he doesn't know how things will work out, he is freed up to continually choose to make the relationship the best it can be, every day.

Rather than asking, "Is marriage going to work out for me?" he essentially asks, "How can I make marriage work out for me?" **The leap of faith into the unknown sometimes has a paradoxical effect—it lands squarely into reality, where we come face-to-face with the concrete consequences of our actions.** Will he enjoy marriage, or won't he? Well, with commitment, Sebastian can understand that the answer to that question hasn't been decided, and it's *him* who decides how good his marriage will be—not fate.

Granted, Kierkegaard's mental model may be overkill for life's more mundane decisions and may take some getting used to if you've routinely favored the rational and the logical. However, it can teach us a lot about approaching life's major inflection points with a wiser, more measured attitude. Kierkegaard says himself on marriage: "Marry and you will regret it; don't marry, you will also regret it; marry or don't marry, you will regret it either way."

So ... What if Regret Was Unavoidable?

To make "informed" decisions, you need information about the costs and likely payoffs. As we've seen, the real world seldom provides crystal-clear information of this kind. We can't always calculate the cost, predict the outcome, or guess how we will do all these things differently in the future, when we ourselves are different.

What if, then, we accept that a certain amount of regret is inevitable in life? What if we consider regret more of an "entry fee" that we all incur in the process of being human beings with free will in a complex and still unfolding world?

We can always learn and gather data, yes. More information can make our "leap" smaller and more manageable. But at some point, there isn't enough data, or there isn't a way to process the available data meaningfully. We need to take that leap that Kierkegaard talks about.

Let's try to condense some of these ideas down into something we can apply practically.

Consider Layla and Ben, who are torn up over the decision to have children or not.

Tip 1: Embrace the fact of regret

Act as though regret is not a sign of poor decision-making or a perfectly avoidable outcome. Instead, take a more measured view and accept that all decisions are necessarily suboptimal in some way or another.

Ben realizes this when he talks to two close friends, one of whom has opted to have children, while the other hasn't. Ben is immediately struck by something: *Both* of them would not change their decision for anything in the world . . . and *both* of them have regrets.

This is important, because it suggests that no matter which path in life we choose, we necessarily close the door on other potential choices. We will never know what life beyond the "other door" may have looked like. This is the nature of choice, and not something we can optimize out of.

Tip 2: Choose your sacrifice

Given that regret is something that will hit most of us sooner or later, try to reframe your questions. Instead of asking, "Which choice has the most positives?" ask instead, "Which *negatives* am I more comfortable with?" In other words, there will be a downside to any choice you make—which downside can you imagine coping with better?

In Ben and Layla's case, they ask, "Which would be the worst regret to have?" They may have to accept the regret of not having children while wishing they did, OR the regret of having children and wishing they didn't. Which regret would be intolerable, and which could be managed over time?

Framed another way, each choice comes with downsides. Being childfree may mean a certain loneliness, doubt, and a feeling of not fitting into family-centric life, but having children may mean financial stress, exhaustion, or relationship damage. Which is worse?

When we choose, we don't just commit to the good—we commit to the bad, too. Acknowledging this, think about which downside you're more willing to deal with. Any major life choice comes with certain sacrifices—which ones are you most willing to make?

Tip 3: Get comfortable with incomplete information

Gather as much as you can, and then just make a choice. It's possible to make effective, sound decisions with incomplete information. Acknowledging these limitations frees you from chasing after some ideal hypothetical situation. It also spares you from getting trapped in endless rumination, worry, and "research" that goes nowhere.

Ben and Layla mull over the decision to have kids for many months. They gather as many facts as they can, but at some point, they deliberately call an end to the fact-finding mission. It's not a sign of personal failure and it's not indecision—it's simply not possessing perfect and total knowledge. And that's okay.

Tip 4: Take the leap of faith

Decide. It's a question of self-determination. As you act, know that you could be making a mistake, and act anyway. Gather the data, analyze the data, but give the final say to your intuition and instincts.

As it happens, Ben and Layla find the decision has already been made for them. There is a surprise pregnancy out of the blue, and they both make the leap together (or rather, they're pushed off the cliff!). Sometimes, we humans flatter ourselves that it is us and us alone in charge of our destinies. Occasionally, we get a glimpse of what may be the larger, more fundamental mechanisms working secretly behind the scenes, whether we understand them or not.

Ben and Layla are surprised to find how calm they feel after they commit to the pregnancy. They feel more vulnerable and uncertain than ever before. Yet paradoxically, their faith in their path is stronger. In the end, these things cannot really be explained. But how many of life's most important decisions have unfolded in just this way?

Plato's Cave

More than two thousand years ago, Plato offered his allegory of prisoners in a cave to make a point about knowledge and reality. In *Republic* he explains it like this:

> "See human beings as though they were in an underground cave-like dwelling with its entrance, a long one, open to the light across the whole width of the cave. They are in it from childhood with their legs and necks in bonds so that they are fixed, seeing only in front of them, unable because of the bond to turn their head all the way around."

Behind these people is a bright fire and a series of puppeteers holding up shapes that cast shadows on the wall. The people in the cave see only the shadows on the wall, and so consider it "reality." They know nothing of the puppeteers, the fire, or the world outside the cave—their world consists of the shadows in front of them.

The following image comes from an FYI article by Tsar Banks and shows how this hypothetical layout might look:

Plato then asks us to imagine what would happen if one of the prisoners escaped and ran out of the cave. He would see the sun, trees, grass, and dozens of other things—not just shadows but *real* objects. What would he then think of the world he once considered his reality? What would he think of the other prisoners back in the cave?

If he went back to tell them, in fact, they may not believe him. Why should they? He would be telling them something that plainly contradicted what they "knew" was reality—they would call him crazy or mistaken. He would consider their view of reality woefully limited and would know they wouldn't change their minds until they, too, stepped outside the cave.

So, what's the point of this strange tale? Granted, Plato's original version contains a few more details and serves as an argument for an illustration of several philosophical concepts that are beyond the scope of this book. However, we can learn something from the simplified version: **People can be trapped in their own "realities" just as surely as the prisoners in the cave can be.** Never knowing reality, they settle for dim, two-dimensional shadows of reality, and they do not know what they do not know.

Though not strictly the own philosopher's aim, Plato's cave allegory has been used to point to the dangers of blindly conforming to majority consensus. If we leave the cave, we are told, we can become one of those enlightened few who interact with the world as it actually is. Plato was no motivational speaker, and his cave analogy wasn't a TED talk about stepping out of your comfort zone. Rather, the exercise points us to the difficulty of acquiring true *knowledge*.

Could there be things in our world that we are taking for granted simply because we have always done so? Could all of our most cherished beliefs be simply shadows on the wall? Could we be chained and imprisoned without knowing that we are, and without realizing that we can turn our head (i.e., change perspectives)?

Appearances are not reality. Our words about reality are not reality. Our cognitive models, beliefs, assumptions, and hopes are not reality, either.

Applied to decision-making, Plato's cave can be a helpful reminder that **the things we take as obvious givens in an equation might not necessarily be true in the way we think they are.** We may take certain premises as correct without really considering if they are, or where they really came from. Plato was a philosopher who was concerned with the reality beneath surface appearances, and his philosophy of "forms" spoke to a deeper "nous" (reason, mind) beyond mankind's temporary enchantment with the more superficial aspects of reality.

Let's try to connect this idea to a real-life example of decision-making with an example.

Sam is wrestling with the decision of what to study in college. On the one hand, he **knows** it's smart to gain in-demand skills that will have the best chance of making him a hirable and attractive employee to future employers, and if he chooses a field like finance or banking, he has a greater chance of earning a lot of money and having much-coveted financial freedom.

On the other hand, he also **knows** that he has considerable artistic talent and would derive satisfaction and meaning from pursuing a career in design or fine art. He **knows** that he wouldn't make much money from this, but it would be more interesting, enjoyable, and in a way, more noble than a run-of-the-mill finance role.

Now, you might read the above and **know** that, of course, the right thing for Sam to do would be to go for the art degree, pursue his dream, and live an authentic, happy life. Or perhaps you **know** that art is a pie-in-the-sky fantasy, and that in today's economic climate, you'd be mad to pass up an opportunity to earn well and secure some financial stability.

There are a million different ways that Sam can make this decision (this book has been about some of them!), but ultimately, Plato would be most curious about all these things that we allegedly *know* to be true in Sam's case. Do we really know these things at all?

To look beyond the superficial, let's ask a few key questions:

Are there any potential "puppeteers" in Sam's life that have been shaping his reality?

Sam may consider how the news he reads, the conversations he has, the social media he engages with, the circles he moves in, the country he's a citizen of, and the family he was raised in shaped his various views, among many other things.

If Sam is frequently having stressful conversations about money with family, constantly watching news about the doomed state of the world, and has heard a few cautionary tales of starving artists, it may well shape his view that "reality" is a place where money is central, difficult to get, and the only thing that affords life meaning or stability.

On the other hand, if he spends all his time following inspirational artists on social media and chatting with a therapist who constantly urges him to find his true self, "reality" may look very different for him.

It's not about whether these worldviews or perspectives are right or wrong—that's a little like getting distracted by the different shapes of the shadows on the wall. Rather, Sam can ask himself how he can step away from the cave entirely. If he removes the strong influence from family, media, culture, and so on, what does he see? What is the reality underneath all these opinions?

Are there any other perspectives he could be neglecting or ignoring?

The prisoners in Plato's cave are chained in such a way as to only ever face forward. Our own mental habits and lazy biases can keep us just as trapped. The wall and the shadows really are there, of course. The problem is that the prisoners have mistakenly come to believe that those shadows are the *only* things that exist. They see nothing else.

In a similar way, Sam can start to realize that there are actually far more perspectives on his dilemma than he might currently be aware of. Is it really true that there are only two options: finance or art? Is it really the case that it's a question of money versus passion, and that a finance job always means security and a creative job always means personal satisfaction? (He should chat with Sebastian about the trap of all-or-nothing thinking!).

While weighing all this up, he realizes that there are a whole host of other occupations and study paths he is discounting out of hand.

He also realizes that it's not quite so black and white—there is a way to *combine* creativity and finance. He could work in advertising or as an animator, or he could become an art dealer.

Are you clearly distinguishing between fact and fiction?

So many of us tell ourselves complicated narratives that "explain" what reality is, promptly forget that we made this story up in the first place, and then proceed as if we were dealing with facts. The shadows on the wall in Plato's cave are just made up. They're just stories. But if people focus on them intently, imbue them with meaning, and assume that they represent the truth, then that's what they become.

Pull back and get really clear about what is genuinely, absolutely factual and what is just your narrative take on something. What is merely opinion, conjecture, interpretation? Crucially, what is *your* opinion, and what is another person's opinion?

When Sam really thinks about it, he realizes that he is basing all his assumptions about the different occupational paths on nothing at all . . . mere hearsay that he has absorbed from friends, family, and his culture at large. When he considers whether he has cold hard evidence for any of his beliefs, he realizes he has none. The things he "knows," in other words, are simply lazy habits and inherited assumptions.

What can he do? For a start, he can seek out real data, but he can also pay careful attention to discern the difference between a mere story or opinion (i.e., a shadow on the wall) versus something that may be genuinely true about the world. So, he hunts down actual statistics and information—job satisfaction surveys, statistics on how many students are employed after a particular program of study, average salary for a given career, projected paths for advancement, and so on.

He carefully considers the strengths and limitations of his own position—not his *opinion* on them—and weighs these up against the opportunities he can see for himself. Of course, there is no way to do this perfectly, and there is some point at which Sam has to admit that there are certain predictions he can't make and outcomes he can't guarantee.

But he can try to explore, to the fullest of his ability, his situation as it really stands. The situation may indeed contain opportunities and risks—but it's worth identifying them as real opportunities and risks rather than mere shadows. **Leaving Plato's cave is certainly a noble task in itself, but our work doesn't end with just identifying reality as accurately as possible—once we see clearly, we are still compelled to act.** This is a little like leaving the cave and discovering not only the nature of the "real world" but also the laws and principles on which it actually runs.

It may not seem like much of a gain to substitute your shadow risks for real risks, but in practice it makes all the difference. Many people spend their lives caught up in dialogue with things that amount to little more than shadows. Their decision-making is limited to the two dimensions of that wall, and in a sense, they have never really made any decision—good or bad—because they have never really been in the world.

The world outside Plato's cave may not be a paradise, and our encountering it may not feel like sublime enlightenment. But seeking it will give us a deeper sense of truth and reality, of meaning, and of a sense of self that is more resilient and robust.

After Sam's long contemplation over his life path, and after mulling over Plato's cave analogy for some time, he comes to an important understanding: If all thought, assumption, explanation, justification, and so on is just like a shadow on a wall, then what *is* "real"? He decides that it's action. Experience. Bringing your will and effort into the world and observing the outcomes, learning, then adjusting your next action.

In a sense, everything covered in this book is a little like a shadow on a wall. Every mental model, idea, and theory covered here is really little more than a few marks scratched onto a page—some things that some people have said. Alternatively, you can think of it as a collection of stories of people who have stepped outside the cave and come to explain to you what they saw. How can we know if they're true? Plato would say there is only one way.

These accounts of the world outside the cave, these mental models, mean nothing until they are **activated**—that is, brought alive in the world (*your* world) by action (*your* action).

And so, we arrive at a paradoxical place: We began our book with one of humanity's most enduring questions—"What ought I to do?" We asked, "What decision-making process will allow me to take the best action?"

In a roundabout way, we discovered that the answer is that *action itself is the best decision-making process.* Any of these models may be right for you, and then again none of them might be. The only way to know for sure is to test them in the laboratory of your own life. It's to step out of the cave and see for yourself what you find. Your best mental model is the one you make for yourself and is the fruit of your own efforts and learning.

Summary

- The vampire analogy: Transformational changes are those that we cannot predict our response to, and so remain as epistemological blind spots. There will also be an element of the unknown to every decision we make, since the decision itself will change us in ways we cannot yet appreciate. You cannot know what you will make of a decision until you make it—and by that time it may be too late.
- In the face of uncertainty, all we can do is honestly acknowledge the gap in our knowledge, seek as much advice and information as we can, and trust the process so that we are willing to commit to whatever decision we do make. Realize

that life is a series of decisions, not just one, and make contingency plans.
- Kierkegaard endorses a deliberate choice to embrace all those things beyond reason and empirical evidence, and to choose to take a leap of faith despite everything. Faith is a decision to act beyond certainty, explanation, or reason—and it may be the key to true freedom. Subjective experience, beyond reason, also has value.
- Plato's cave is an allegory that warns us of the danger of too readily accepting ideas, beliefs, and opinions as reality. You can be trapped in a false "reality" and not know it. Appearances are not reality. Our cognitive models, beliefs, assumptions, and hopes are not reality, either, so we need to constantly seek evidence. Be as clear as possible about what is fact and what isn't, and don't automatically assume that your current understanding is all there is.

www.ingramcontent.com/pod-product-compliance
Lightning Source LLC
Chambersburg PA
CBHW060606080526
44585CB00013B/701